PEACE AND CO
JOURNAL OF PEACE

CW01651776

Volume 6, Number 3

SPECIAL ISSUE

Millennium Issue I: Envisioning Peaceful Futures

SUBSCRIBER INFORMATION

Peace and Conflict: Journal of Peace Psychology is published four times a year and subscriptions for the 2000 volume are available on a calendar-year basis. In the United States and Canada, per-volume rates are US $35 for individuals and US $200 for institutions; in other countries, per-volume rates are US $65 for individuals and US $230 for institutions. Send subscription orders and information requests to the Journal Subscription Department, Lawrence Erlbaum Associates, Inc., 10 Industrial Avenue, Mahwah, NJ 07430–2262.

Electronic: Full print subscribers to Volume 6, 2000 are entitled to receive the electronic version free of charge. *Electronic only* subscriptions are available at a reduced subscription price. Please visit the lEA website at http://www.erlbaum.com for complete information.

Address changes: Members of Division 48 of the APA should contact Adele Schaefer, Division Services Office, APA, 750 First St. NE, Washington DC 20002–4242. Direct subscribers should contact Lawrence Erlbaum Associates, Inc., at the aforementioned address. Address changes should include the mailing label or a facsimile. Claims for missing issues cannot be honored beyond 4 months after mailing date. Duplicate copies cannot be sent to replace issues not delivered due to failure to notify publisher of change of address.

This journal is abstracted or indexed in *PsycINFO/Psychological Abstracts, Political Science Abstracts, International Political Science Abstracts, Peace Research Abstracts Journal, Public Affairs Information Service, International Bibliography of the Social Sciences, Sociological Abstracts, Social Services Abstracts* and *Linguistics & Language Behavior Abstracts.* Microform copies of this journal are available through Bell & Howell Information and Learning, P.O. Box 1346, Ann Arbor, MI 48106–1346.

PEACE AND CONFLICT: JOURNAL OF PEACE PSYCHOLOGY, *6*(3), 187–191

INTRODUCTION

Envisioning Peaceful Futures

Milton Schwebel
Graduate School of Applied & Professional Psychology
Rutgers University

The new century invites reflection on the future: whether and by what means the 21st century can be less bloody and more benign than the 20th. The purpose of this special issue is to seek a balanced view that neither ignores the harsh realities of today's world nor drains us of hope for the future.

> [M]ore than ever I see hope as a necessity. Hope enables constructive involvement, which in turn nourishes hope, in a benign reciprocal process.
>
> M. Brewster Smith (1999, p. 14)

New Year's Day of year 2000 (Y2K) has come and gone and the world has remained unchanged. To the dismay and embarrassment of soothsayers of doom, none of the dire predictions materialized.

Yet, the occasion, much more than a run of the mill New Year's Day, encourages pause for reflection—a time to take stock, asking challenging questions about our collective future. As an emerging global society, where does the current trajectory suggest that we are headed? Will the history of the 21st century be bloodied by ethnopolitical warfare as the 20th was by wars between nations? Will nuclear fission, that genie that can't be put back into the bottle, cast a dark shadow over the world in this century as it did during the second half of the last one? Will the seeds of violent class struggle continue to be sewn within nations, with ever-wider gaps in wealth and income between the affluent and the middle and lower classes, and

Requests for reprints should be sent to Milton Schwebel, Graduate School of Applied & Professional Psychology, Rutgers University, 152 Frelinghuysen Road, Piscataway, NJ 08854–8085. E-mail: mschwebe@rci.rutgers.edu

will they be sewn between nations and regions, widening even further the chasm between the rich nations of the northern hemisphere and the poor of the southern? Will malnutrition, starvation, disease, and illiteracy blight so much of the world, whereas profit, and the production of millionaires, are the highlights of affluent nations? Will the inequality and injustice suffered by oppressed minorities and women that fill many pages of 20th century history, also mar the 21st? Will children still be used as soldiers and prostitutes, and will rape continue to be employed as an instrument of war and a trophy of victory?

Even in the more formal, less affective terms of a taxonomy of ethnopolitical violence (Suedfeld, 1999), containing among its ten categories, "revolutionary terrorism" and "populist persecution," the very topics themselves sound forbidding, and the obstacles to peace seemingly intractable.

The weight of the aforementioned questions, especially one following another, can drive psychologists to seek areas of research less fraught with mine fields of despair. Yet, there is enough change in the world to give cause for hope: peaceful transition in the Philippines and South Africa; negotiated settlements in nearly decimated Nicaragua and Salvador; and progress, snail-like though it is, in the Middle East and Northern Ireland. There *has* been progress in the struggles for social justice and equality for women and minorities in many countries. Increasingly people *are* becoming aware of the effects of war on children, and the outcry of citizens against the monolithic sway of the World Trade Organization is but one instance of many where people are organizing and speaking out in their own interests. Furthermore, because of its development in the last half of the 20th century, psychology's "methods of research are more powerful, its experience with the affairs of real life richer, and interdisciplinary political psychology, in particular, is better equipped to contribute to understanding the problems concerning war and peace" (Smith, 1999, p.13). Examples of those contributions, especially to knowledge about the prevention of violent conflict, may be seen, among others, in the work of Cairns (1996), Deutsch (Bunker & Rubin, 1995), Kelman (1999), McKay (1998), Osgood (1962), Staub (1999), Wessells and Winter (1998), and White (1970).

Because hope is so essential to continued effort to move to more peaceful ways of life, those engaged in the fields of peace and political psychology need to maintain a balanced view. They need to bear in mind the positive aspects of recent history and current developments along with the heavy weight of negatives.

To obtain a balanced view of the future, it seemed desirable to publish an article that presents a critical vision of future relationships among the people of the world, along with commentaries representing the reactions, and perhaps alternative visions, of peace scholars and scholar–activists from diverse regions of the globe. By "critical vision" we mean neither a fantasized version of the future, without any empirical roots, nor a forecast or prediction weighted down heavily by the state of the world as it is at the start of the 21st century. The area between those two is our notion of "vision," soaring high with two feet planted firmly, lofty ideas subject to empirical validation. For goal-directed psychologists and other social scientists, such a critical vision could serve as a paradigm, or in more poetic terms, a guiding star.

More specifically, we had in mind the future prospects for a culture of peace. With that concept an integral part of United Nations Educational, Scientific, and Cultural Organization (UNESCO) programming, and with the United Nations (UN) dedicating the year 2000 and the first decade of the new century to education for a culture of peace, we thought it useful to examine the outlook for its realization in the coming years, slow though it may be.

To undertake that difficult assignment, we invited sociologist and peace researcher, Elise Boulding, professor emeritus at Dartmouth and former president of the International Peace Research Association, who had just completed her latest book, *Cultures of Peace: The Hidden Side of History* (2000). In addition, we invited scholars and activists from a dozen nations other than the United States to react to and comment on Dr. Boulding's article. The seven who accepted and submitted articles are from Canada, Mexico, the Philippines, South Africa, Uganda, United Kingdom, and the UN. Finally, Dr. Boulding wrote a response to the seven commentaries.

In her article, A New Chance for Human Peaceableness?, Boulding speaks of the optimism generated among nongovernmental organizations (NGOs) by the UN Declaration of a Year and a Decade of Education for a Culture of Peace and Nonviolence for the Children of the World. She sees it as opening the possibility of a "paradigm shift from dominance to mutualism in both interpersonal and interstate relations." Outlining the negatives (e.g., NGO turfism) and positives (e.g., truth commissions) on the world scene, she highlights some of the perplexing challenges that confront us.

Four authors of commentaries, all from Third World nations, and all women, present much less than optimistic outlooks on the future. Responding to Boulding, Cheryl de la Rey of South Africa reminds us that how we perceive future prospects depends on the part of the world we live in and conditions there in regard to poverty, equality, and violence. Caroline Lamwaka of Uganda says "mutualism" as opposed to "dominance" is a grand vision, but considering human behavior, as for example, in the recent bloody and frustrating history of Uganda, she wonders if it is possible. Ursula Oswald Spring of Mexico says that if there is a chance for human peaceableness we must first resolve the pervasive problems of poverty, violence, ecological destruction, and discrimination, especially against women, children, ethnic and minority groups, and the elderly. For Mary Soledad L. Perpiñan, peace doesn't mean acquiescence to an unjust patriarchal system of economic, ecological, and sexual exploitation and cultural and religious oppression, and, wanting to have hope, she proposes five programmatic actions.

In the fifth commentary, Adam Curle of the United Kingdom, an author and activist with many years of experience in Third World nations, shares with the first four authors a very mixed outlook on the future, pointing out that the advances in technology and marketing that have strengthened the culture of peace in recent years have done the same for the malign culture of violence. Peter Suedfeld of Canada, challenging Boulding's optimism, questions her interpretations of past and current events and her "extrapolations from these to the future," and questions, too, whether some self-designated peace-enhancing groups really do what they claim. In the final commentary, David Adams of UNESCO, without minimizing the enormous obstacles, brings hope to the commentaries by focusing on the mission of transforming a culture of war to one of peace, presenting actions that are intended to facilitate the transformation. This special issue comes to a close with Boulding's personal and open-minded response to the commentaries. However, we hope that it does not end with her words, as I explain later.

More than a dozen people were involved in the process of producing this special issue, among them some whose advice I sought at the outset: Dan Christie, Morton Deutsch, Herbert Kelman, Susan Fiske, Doris Miller, Brewster Smith, Ethel Tobach, Richard Wagner, and Michael Wessells. Then there were the eight contributors, as well as my assistant, Michelle McNamara, and our production editor, Rick Maffei.

Now, we propose *your* active involvement, and not simply as a critical reader. Before reading the articles that follow and then again after you have read them, consider the following questions. What is *your* critical vision of the future of the world in respect to just and harmonious relationships among people, nations, and regions? As a psychologist, or other social scientist, what are *your* expectations for the future and the assumptions on which they are based? If you care to share them, we will consider them for publication in the journal.

REFERENCES

Boulding, E. (2000). *Cultures of peace: The hidden side of history.* Syracuse, NY: Syracuse University Press.

Bunker, B. B., Rubin, J. Z., & Associates (1995). *Conflict, cooperation & justice: Essays inspired by the work of Morton Deutsch.* San Francisco: Jossey-Bass

Cairns, E. (1996). *Children and political violence.* Oxford, England: Basil Blackwell.

Kelman, H. C. (1999). Interactive problem solving as a metaphor for international conflict resolution: Lessons for the policy process. *Peace and Conflict: Journal of Peace Psychology, 5*(4), 201–218.

McKay, S.(1998). From war to peace: Women and societal reconstruction. In L. Lorentzen & J. Turpin (Eds.), *The women and war reader* (pp. 348–362). New York: New York University Press.

Osgood, C. E. (1962). *An alternative to war and surrender.* Urbana: University of Illinois Press.

Smith, M. B. (1999). Political psychology and peace: A half-century perspective. *Peace and Conflict: Journal of Peace Psychology, 5*(1), 17–22.

Staub, E.(1999). The origins and prevention of genocide, mass killing, and other collective violence. *Peace and Conflict: Journal of Peace Psychology, 5*(4), 303–336.

Suedfeld, P. (1999). Toward a taxonomy of ethnopolitcal violence: Is collective killing by any other name still the same? *Peace and Conflict: Journal of Peace Psychology, 5*(4), 349–356.

Wessells, M., & Winter, D. D. (1998). The Graca Machel/UN study on the effects of war on children. *Peace and Conflict: Journal of peace Psychology, 4*(4; Special Issue), 319–428.

White, R. (1970). *Nobody wanted war: Misperception in Vietnam and other wars.* Garden City, NY: Doubleday.

The leaders of the nuclear weapon states today risk very much being judged by future historians as having been unworthy of their age, of not having taken advantage of opportunities so perilously won at such great sacrifice and cost, of re-igniting nuclear arms races around the world, of condemning mankind to live under a cloud of perpetual anxiety. This is not a legacy worthy of the human race. This is not the world that I want to bequeath to my children and grandchildren. It's simply intolerable.

General George Lee Bailey, March 1999

PEACE AND CONFLICT: JOURNAL OF PEACE PSYCHOLOGY, *6*(3), 193–215

A New Chance for Human Peaceableness?

Elise Boulding
Professor Emeritus of Sociology
Dartmouth College

The millennial optimism being generated among nongovernmental organizations (NGOs) in the global civil society by the advent of the year 2000, and the United Nations Declaration of a Year and Decade of Education for a Culture of Peace and Nonviolence for the Children of the World, opens the possibility of a paradigm shift from dominance to mutualism in both interpersonal and interstate relations. Multiple year 2000 peace initiatives by NGOs present them with the challenge of a shift from turfism to collaboration in peacebuilding. Truth commissions offer new opportunities for peace work. Peace movements are learning to apply interactive problem-solving skills as they shift from protest to peace practitioner roles in war-torn areas. The power of the social imagination to envision peaceful futures is critical to all these efforts.

The century started off so promisingly. In May 1899 Tsar Nicholas and the Queen of the Netherlands convened the Hague Peace Conference to put an end to war as an instrument of national policy and to replace it with diplomacy as a means for settlement of disputes among states. The International Peace Bureau—an early forerunner of the later flowering of nongovernmental organizations (NGOs)—had been founded a few years before. It all began with the series of world fairs starting with the great London Exposition of 1851, bringing scientists, educators, social reform advocates, and people from the world of arts together in a new type of exchange and networking. New ideas began emerging from an enthusiastic study of international law and arbitration procedures. This released new peace movement energies and helped create a new international mindset that, it was thought, would render war obsolete.

Developments in the succeeding century—the International Court of Justice, then the League of Nations, and finally the United Nations (UN)—kept being

---

Requests for reprints should be sent to Elise Boulding, 44 East Plain Street, Wayland, MA 01778.

rudely interrupted: first by World War I, then World War II, and in the most recent decades by intrastate and interstate wars on every continent. World War I itself has been referred to as "the original sin of our dreadful century, the blood-polluted source of all our sorrows. From its oozing wounds issued the triumphs of Bolshevism and Fascism; worldwide depression; and military innovations like large-scale bombardments, chemical warfare, and the soldierly conviction that 'mass annihilation is the best route to victory' (Schama, 1996, pp. 96–99). Yet hope and despair have surged along parallel tracks right up to the year 2000. In the face of the violence humankind seeks to control, hope has a durability and generates a continuing capacity for positive social action that deserves the utmost respect.

It is not insignificant that in the middle of this century (1954, to be exact), the Council of Europe, struggling to rebuild a war-torn continent, gave a special award to the Dutch historian–sociologist Fred Polak for his *Image of the Future* (1961). This path-breaking historical work portrayed the capacity to imagine a future different and better than the present as a key human trait, and one that empowered those who envision the better to act on the vision to bring it to fruition. Polak cited historical evidence that societies without dreams of the future go into decline, and those societies that engage in positive imaging harness their actions to the image, becoming vital agents of human betterment.

Polak's book was an early signal of important new fields of study that have generated new social movements that continue their unfolding today: futurism, peace, development, environment, gender roles, and human rights. Although the fields developed separately, they are increasingly understood as interdependent, and they all depend on that basic capacity to look through and beyond overwhelming problems of the present to a different and better set of lifeways for the planet.

WHAT HISTORY TEACHES US

Precisely because we seem to have such overwhelming evidence of a human inclination toward violence and war from the very century that was supposed to be an end to war, it is of the utmost importance that we take a fresh look at the human experience over time, to see if violence is indeed inevitable. The first thing we discover is that the cards are stacked in favor of a story of war-making through the centuries. Wars and conquests are depicted in song, story, and in highly visible monuments erected by winners to celebrate their victories over the centuries. No continent is without these records. Yet, in Bernhard Grun's *Timetables of History* (Grun, 1975), tabulating events year by year from 501 B.C. (and by half-centuries before that, starting at 4000 B.C.), only one column entry lists wars won and lost. The other column entries include literature and theater; religion, philosophy and learning; visual arts; music; science, technology, and growth; and daily life. The peaceful activities far outweigh the battles.

Yes, there is substantial, factual evidence that humans spend most of their time in essentially peaceful activities. Polak reminds us that humans have also spent a lot of time visioning and dreaming about a better way of life than they currently experience. This dreaming, which might be thought of as escapist, is actually energizing. Furthermore, the most unlikely societies do it. Even warrior societies dreamed of the joys of peaceful lifeways. The Vikings dreamed of the Great Hall of Asgard, where former enemies feasted and sang to each other; the Greek warriors dreamed of the Elysian Fields, where fighters hung their swords in trees and walked arm in arm declaiming poetry and philosophy to one another. Muslim warriors dreamed of paradise as a garden in the desert, nurturing all comers.

The history of utopian social movements, putting utopian dreams into practice, is a long and adventurous one. It ranges from early Christian desert communes to the socialist and New Age utopias of Europe, the Americas, Asia, and Africa. In practice, the utopian ventures of each century have had practical spinoffs for the larger society in terms of new opportunities, the development of new skills, and the modeling of new types of human relationships.

Another counterweight to the prevailing view of history as the story of battles won and lost is the story of peace movements through the centuries. Every century has had its movement to bring war and violence to an end. Gene Sharp's magnificent *Politics of Nonviolent Action* and more recent documentation of strategic nonviolence through the centuries by associates of the Albert Einstein Institution under Gene Sharp's direction (McCarthy & Sharp, 1997; Sharp, 1973) have amply made the point that strategically directed nonviolence has repeatedly overcome violence and oppression in the human experience.

The history of nonviolence is the history of human creativity. The practice of creating zones of peace in the midst of violence goes back many centuries and is found on all continents. The inventiveness of peace movements was particularly evident during the wars of the European Middle Ages. The church contributed by declaring certain areas around churches and marketplaces as zones of peace where there could be no fighting on certain days of the week. Throughout the centuries, including in our own time, the capacity of local citizens' groups to declare certain areas as zones of peace with no weapons allowed has reduced the carnage of guerilla warfare.

The rebalancing of our image of human activity in the past, and of our capacity to see the full diversity of human happenings in the present, is coming about with renewed vigor as activists draw on the positive energies of millennialism, as we will see later. This rebalancing has also been an important part of the work of the United Nations Educational, Scientific, and Cultural Organization (UNESCO) since its founding as part of the United Nations in 1945, with the constitutional mandate to construct the defenses of peace in the minds of women and men. It was in 1986, during the UN International Year of Peace, that the Spanish National Commission for UNESCO convened the Seville gathering of biologists, psychologists, ethnologists, geneticists, and others to provide a solid underpinning for Margaret Mead's famous pre-World War II essay, "Warfare is only an invention, not a biological necessity." The Seville Statement concludes that humans are not genetically programmed for war, that war is not a biological necessity but a social invention, and peace must be invented to replace it (Adams, 1991). Three years later, UNESCO held an International Congress on Peace in the Minds of Men (sic) in Yamassoukro, Ivory Coast, at which the concept of *peace culture*, focused on values and behaviors and social institutions within every society which could make peace a sustainable human condition, was clearly articulated.

The Yamassoukro conference was a powerful occasion, deeply affecting everyone there (this author included), and laid the groundwork for the UN International Year (2000) and Decade (2001–2010) of Education for a Culture of Peace and Nonviolence for the Children of the World. The UN declaration establishing this Decade is, in fact, a revolutionary document, for developing a worldwide culture of peace requires a major reorganization of human society. According to Federico Mayor, Director General of UNESCO (Mayor, 1996), it "means a transition from societies dominated by the State, sole organizer of security in a dangerous world, to the civil society of everyday life ... it must welcome and promote citizen participation in national and international affairs. It must construct peace in the minds of men and women by linking the individual to global networks of shared interests and local communities to the international."

Needless to say, women, children, and all oppressed minorities have special roles in bringing about a social transformation away from structures of domination toward relationships of authentic and practical equality for everyone. Family life, child-rearing practices, and the quality of neighborhood relations, as well as opportunities for education, access to social services, jobs, and resources all need to be reexamined in the context of the social structures and human relationships required to sustain a peace culture.

My own working definition of peace culture is: a mosaic of identities, attitudes, values, beliefs, and institutional patterns that lead people to live nurturantly with one another and the earth itself without the aid of structured power differentials, to deal creatively with their differences, and share their resources. For the most part, peaceableness and aggression coexist as clusters of attitudes and behaviors present in varying proportions in most societies, reflecting twin basic human needs for both bonding and autonomy. However, we can find islands of peace culture in sectors of every society: communities dedicated to a life of nonviolence, peace NGOs, the historic peace churches, and peace fellowships within every faith tradition. Music, art, dance, theater, poetry—and sheer play—are all expressions of peace culture when they reflect humanity's sense of beauty and reverence for life.

Peace cultures as separate entities can be found in relatively isolated indigenous communities that handle conflict with an easy but practiced nonviolence. The hunter–gatherer, rain forest-dwelling Mbuti in the northeastern part of former

Zaire (may they survive current warfare in the region!) are one among a number of indigenous peoples who carefully raise their children to live at peace with all living things, as described in Bruce Bonta's bibliography of peaceful peoples (Bonta, 1993). Indigenous peoples have the advantage of never having lost their first teacher, nature. Many lessons in interdependence are taught by the natural world to those who watch and listen. Introducing nature as teacher to the schoolchildren of the world, by stepping outside the classroom into the local lifeworld, may be one of the best ways of strengthening the peace culture of any society.

Women's culture, passed down from generation to generation in familial households, has traditionally been the carrier of peaceful behaviors, and not only because women are the bearers and rearers of children and keepers of the family home base. From tribal societies to kingdoms, they have tended to be married off to men in neighboring communities to serve as communication channels and unofficial peacemakers. In the modern world, they continue to be the primary family caregivers, but with the development of women's NGOs from the middle of the 19th century, they have brought an inventiveness and creativity to public peacemaking that is finally being documented, though it was long ignored (Boulding, 1992). Women, like Buddhist general systems theorist and ecopeace activist Joanna Macy, systems modeling farmer and professor Donella Meadows, Kenyan biologist and founder of the Green Belt Movement Wangari Maathai, Indian physicist ecosystem-saver Vandana Shiva, and Swedish Disarmament Ambassador Alva Myrdal, have all been able to link peace, the environment, development, and human rights both in their conceptual analysis of world problems and in practical on-the-ground solutions. Women have led in the development of peace education in schools worldwide. The Women's International League for Peace and Freedom, founded during World War I, and the Women's Environment and Development Organization have worked both locally, with governments, and at the UN on disarmament, development, and environmental issues, always bringing an otherwise lacking expertise to men's decision-making bodies.

The men's movement that has supported these feminist activities (Boulding, 2000) points to a new partnership between women and men in both family and public life, a partnership that is a key element in the contemporary development of a more sustainable peace culture.

PARADIGM SHIFT? THE RISE OF NGOS

Are we undergoing a paradigm shift in our view of the role of power and dominance in our social institutions and our institutions of governance? Is mutualism replacing dominance in models of human relationships? Certainly there are a great variety of equity and interdependence-focused movements in every sector of our society, as Gordon Fellman and others have pointed out (Fellman, 1998). How much society-wide new social learning is going on, and how much fragmentation and splintering? One can paint either a bleak or an optimistic picture of the present. On the one hand, local violence is increasing, whether in the schools of the United States or intergroup violence in the Balkans, the Caucasus, parts of Africa, and South Asia. The world arms trade flourishes, and nuclear disarmament negotiations have practically ground to a halt. Global megacorporations are swallowing other megacorporations, respecting no boundaries as they mine the earth's resources, damage its environments, and exploit many of its peoples. States are helpless. The major powers can no more control global corporations than can the smallest of states. A westernized mass media exports a violent and greedy consumer culture to the rest of the world. The rich grow richer and the poor grow poorer.

On the other hand, civil society around the world is flourishing as never before. The 20,000 globe-spanning NGOs representing a new local-to-local interconnectedness as humans pursue humanitarian, cultural, scientific, and recreational concerns independently of the governmental agendas of the countries they live in, hold real promise of human betterment. For the first half of this century, NGOs tended to be based in the West and are still to a degree thought of as a form of "civil society imperialism" in southern countries. This has been particularly true as NGOs have been prone to their own parochialism and insensitive to actual local needs in the regions where they carry out projects. However, more and more NGOs are now originating in the Two-Thirds World and spreading to the One-Third World. NGOs are important because they have a freedom of movement and command knowledge resources that governments cannot command. Disparaging NGOs is easy, but it can also be said that they are going through a time of major new social learning, a time of awakening to the great diversity and complexity that underlie the surface glibness of a rich and variegated global culture that is poorly understood in the One-Third World, where "global" is often primarily thought of as "Western." The revolution in communication that the Internet has brought about divides even as it unites because there is so much more to communication than simply passing around messages and data. The Internet is sometimes described as a modern Tower of Babel, where everyone is talking and no one understands.

The "10,000 societies"[1] or ethnies that crisscross the boundaries of the 189 states of the international system are poorly integrated into the 20,000-strong NGO system. However, the new development of ethnic NGOs is making possible a dialogue that brings hitherto unrecognized social, spiritual, and environmental values

---

[1]The "10,000 societies" is a term loosely used by some anthropologists. According to Nietschmann, there are "5,000 distinct communities in the contemporary world (that) might claim that they are national peoples on grounds that they share common ancestry, institutions, beliefs, language, and territory." Quoted in Ted Gurr & James Scarrett, *Minorities at Risk: A Global Survey.* Human Rights Quarterly, 11, 1989, p. 375.

into the global discourse and a new knowledge about earth as a complex of interdependent living systems. At the same time, a new consciousness is developing among some of the elite of the urban-based technological society, accompanied by a conviction that humans are on the threshold of a new development of their capacity for, awareness of, and relationship with currents that reach beyond the earth into the cosmos.[2] People who develop this awareness lose interest in the consumer society. Not a few of them put their energies into exploring how to rescue humans from the grip of violence, war, and greed. Another source of new levels of awareness about the human condition comes from interfaith groups, such as the World Council of Religion and Peace, the newly revived one-century-old World Parliament of Religions, and its offshoot, the Interfaith Peace Council. These bodies build on the powerful but widely ignored teachings on peace, nonviolence, inward spiritual development, and respect for and nurture of all life that are present in all religious traditions.

The peace, environment, development, and human rights NGOs have contributed much to the development of values, scientific knowledge, institutional structures of law, and regulatory systems, and problem-solving skills that should be useful in violence-prone societies that seem helpless to control the temptations to exploitation and warfare. Yet, in a way, these NGO contributions to social betterment have remained oddly disconnected from one another. The tendency to turfism among NGOs has made relations between organizations working on similar tracks competitive rather than cooperative. Relations among NGOs on related tracks, particularly the peace, environment, development, and human rights groups, are even more distant. Opportunities for serious collaborative reflection by NGO activists on the ways in which their activities are interdependent, on how each can most constructively take account of and relate to the others, are far too few. Thus, opportunities for mutually beneficial cooperation are lost over and over again.

Not only are opportunities lost for collaboration in the field, but opportunities are lost for collaboration in approaches to governments and the UN. Although the NGO consultative group on disarmament does represent collaborative efforts among peace NGOs, and similar networks exist for environmental, development, and human rights NGOs, there is no comparable body that brings all four groups together. To date, the idea of a paradigm shift toward conceptualizing human relations in terms of empowerment and mutual nurturance and away

---

[2]In the United States, the Institute of Noetic Sciences, the California Institute of Integral Studies, and the Center for the Story of the Universe, all in California, exemplify the development of this new consciousness. In England, the journal Resurgence gives broad coverage to this type of development. Joanna Macy and Molly Young Brown's *Coming Back to Life: Practices to Reconnect Our Lives, Our World*, Gabriola Island, BC, Canada: New Society Publishers, 1998, provides a good overview of this unusual field.

from dominance and conquest seems more elusive than ever. If there is such a shift, it is not happening in enough human minds.

THE MILLENNIUM

Will this change as more and more NGOs catch "millennial fever"? Although the year 2000 is a calendric artifact of the Christian calendar, that calendar has been adopted as a useful global dating system and has already created expectations for an apocalyptic break in the familiar social order. Similar "breaches in time" are found in the histories of many civilizations. If the emotional energy currently generated by millennialist hopes can be harnessed to practical projects of social learning and social transformation on the part of the NGOs, the grass-roots organizations (GROs), and the ethnies that make up the global civil society, there could indeed be a major shift away from the militarized power paradigm that has prevailed in the face of the fractionated peacebuilding efforts to date.

Two recent landmark achievements of NGOs working with states, intergovernmental bodies, and the UN itself fuel the optimism of this historical moment: the International Treaty to Ban Landmines, signed in 1996 by 123 states in the face of opposition by the major powers, and the Treaty to Establish an International Criminal Court, signed in 1998 by 107 states, again in the face of opposition by the major powers. In each case, there had been a hard-working coalition of about 1,000 NGOs acting more or less collaboratively to bring the treaties into actual functioning existence. When the goals are specific enough, NGOs can collaborate!

Current millennialist peace efforts began with the Hague Appeal for Peace 1999, organized by a coalition of about 600 NGOs to renew the failed original Hague Appeal of 1899. It did indeed bring 1,000 NGOs together at the Hague, and something short of 10,000 people were present; but in terms of achievements, it has been labeled as "peace tourism" by at least one experienced peace NGO. Size and logistics overpowered substance, and workable plans could not emerge that represented the actual capabilities of participating NGOs. However, it was a first, and the process of learning how to create coalitions of groups that draw on the special resources and abilities of each, on a global scale, will be a long slow one. Bureaucratic shortcuts and compromises with representatives of the major powers resulted in the failure of the Hague Assembly to condemn the NATO bombing at that moment going on in Yugoslavia—surely a glaring failure to live up to the purposes of the conference, which included the furthering of disarmament, conflict prevention, and transformation, and the launching of efforts to create a culture of peace to deal with the root causes of war! The peace tourism label was given in criticism of the fact that by far the largest number of attendees came form the United States, and there were very few participants from the Two-Thirds World.

The now-sobered participants may try harder in other year 2000 initiatives, such as Abolition 2000 (also represented at the Hague Appeal), a coalition of 1,300 NGOs on six continents that calls itself a Global Network to Eliminate Nuclear Weapons and has a very solid group of scientific NGOs at its core. Then there is Jubilee 2000, a global coalition of faith communities, supporting debt forgiveness for the Two-Thirds World, drawing on Hebrew teachings regarding the systematic removal of economic and social inequities every 50 years. Many NGOs are part of both Abolition 2000 and Jubilee 2000—clearly the issues of war and poverty are linked in the minds of many. The Earth Charter 2000 is not organized on as large a scale, but this network of NGOs brings together all the issues of violence and exploitation of the earth and its peoples in a covenant that it hopes to bring to the UN 2000 Millennial General Assembly with signatures from thousands of people on every continent.

THE CULTURE OF PEACE DECADE

The UN General Assembly in 2000 will certainly be a major event and will launch the Year and Decade of Education for a Culture of Peace and Nonviolence for the Children of the World—another opportunity for massive peace development activities on the part of NGOs—if they are ready. The special value at this moment in time of the peace culture concept is that it can conceptually unite the whole range of existing NGOs. An NGO is not necessarily an embodiment of peace culture, though it may be, but in its way of working, it can contribute to the development of peace culture.

Many NGOs have been making pledges to focus their work during the 2000–2010 period in ways appropriate to their sphere of competence, on the development of peace culture. Furthermore, the pledge concept reaches right down to the individual. Commitment 2000 is a pledge drafted by a gathering of Nobel Laureats being distributed by various NGOs and being signed by individuals around the world at the time of this writing.[3] Their names will appear on the Internet Web site www.unesco.org/manifesto2000 and will be presented to the Millennial UN General Assembly. The pledge reads as follows:

> Recognizing my share of responsibility for the future of humanity, especially for today's children and those of future generations, I pledge—in my daily life, in my family, my work, my community, my country and my region—to:
>
> 1. *Respect the life* and dignity of every person without discrimination or prejudice.

[3]The primary distributor for Commitment 2000 is the International Fellowship of Reconciliation, Spoorstraat 38, 1815 BK Alkmaar, The Netherlands.

2. *Practice active nonviolence*, rejecting violence in all its forms: physical, sexual, psychological, economical, and social, in particular toward the most deprived and vulnerable such as children and adolescents.

3. *Share my time and material resources* in a spirit of generosity to put an end to exclusion, injustice, and political and economic oppression.

4. *Defend freedom of expression and cultural diversity,* giving preference always to dialogue and listening rather than fanaticism, defamation, and the rejection of others.

5. *Promote consumer behaviour that is responsible* and development practices that respect all forms of life and preserve the balance of nature on the planet.

6. *Contribute to the development of my community,* with the full participation of women and respect for democratic principles, in order to create together new forms of solidarity.

The pledge closes with space for individual signers to state what will be their personal contribution to the promotion of a culture of peace and nonviolence. The device of pledging introduces the element of actual behavior change. The use of the term peacebuilding emphasizes that developing a culture of peace is a *process* and involves developing the skills of conflict resolution, mediation, and peacemaking.

This emphasis on behavioral skills has been sadly lacking in many of the NGOs committed to furthering the related spheres of peace, development, environment, and human rights. The focus has tended to be on the policies and institutions needed rather than on how differences can be handled. The evolution of listening dialogues can lead to new perceptions of the problems at issue and, therefore, to new solutions. The International Peace Research Association (IPRA), for example, which was founded to advance interdisciplinary research on the conditions of peace and the causes of war and other forms of violence, has 16 commissions on various aspects of the peace problematique but is only now recognizing the importance of the *practice* of conflict resolution. Interestingly, the new initiative comes from IPRA's African affiliate, the African Peace Research Association, which is now networking peacemaking capabilities across the continent and promoting peace practitioner training in African universities. Similarly, activities are now being considered by IPRA as a joint initiative of IPRA members to deal with increasing culture clashes between peoples on the opposite shores of the Mediterranean, the European, and the African-Arab.

At the same time, psychologists, both within IPRA and in their own professional associations, have done outstanding work in developing practical models of listening dialogue for parties in conflict. Herbert Kelman (1986) of Harvard University, building on earlier work by John Burton, has been one of the pioneers in interactive problem solving. Kelman has facilitated such dialogues between Palestinians and Israelis for many years (Kelman, 1986). Now there are a number of universities and institutes across Europe, and in Asia and Africa as well as in the Americas, that provide training in conflict resolution, mediation, and conflict transformation, and offer hope for a wider distribution of these skills in the future. Dispute settlement has emerged as an independent profession with its own professional organizations, but it is sad that the field is only now being recognized by NGOs in related fields. Major gaps remain.

PEACE TEAMS AND PEACE SERVICES

To their credit, a few peace activist NGOs saw the need for such training early on, inspired by the Shanti Sena, or peace armies that were part of the Gandhian movement in India. This led to the concept of global civilian peace services and to the development of a number of NGO peace team initiatives since the 1970s. Peace Brigades International and a dozen other NGOs maintain unarmed, highly trained peace teams in Africa, Asia, the Americas, and Europe. They create safe spaces in the midst of violence, where dialogue can take place; carry messages between hostile parties; offer nonviolent strategies for dealing with conflicts; and work for conflict transformation. A parallel set of NGOs, such as International Alert and the Institute for Multitrack Diplomacy, practice preventive diplomacy in areas that threaten to become conflict hot spots. The Swedish Peace Team Forum, consisting of 30 Swedish peacebuilding NGOs, works to expand such peace services. A 1997 conference in Gripsholm, Sweden, cosponsored by the Forum and the Swedish Ministry of Foreign Affairs (a good example of NGO–government cooperation), was the occasion for establishing contacts between a new NGO network, the European Center for Conflict Prevention, and similar networks around the world. The European Center's 1998 *International Directory on Prevention and Management of Conflict*[4] is an excellent guide to NGOs supporting peace teams on every continent, as well as to other peacebuilding NGOs. The center also publishes a valuable quarterly newsletter. Transcend, a computer network of peace scholars and practitioners that offers on-site and in-person training in conflict transformation, started by Johan Galtung in the 1990s, is another important resource for peace services.

As of this writing, there is a strong new move afoot among the rapidly growing peace team and peace services NGOs to expand teams in size to increase their effectiveness. Already widespread, they are to be found in such places as the Balkans (including Kosova); in Chiapas, Mexico; Colombia; Cuba; Guatemala; Haiti; Honduras; Nicaragua; Palestine–Israel; Puerto Rico; and East Timor. Special

[4]The *International Directory on Prevention and Management of Conflict* is published by the European Center for Conflict Prevention, P.O. Box 14069, 3508 SC Utrecht, The Netherlands.

training, including training for local women, are currently being held in a number of countries on every continent. Many of these groups are affiliated with the International Fellowship of Reconciliation and some with Quakers, Mennonites, and other faith groups.[5] Local grass-roots women's groups are forming their own healing and peacemaking groups in the very countries where the worst genocide has occurred and are being supported by foundations such as the Global Fund for Women.

PEACE CULTURE AT THE STATE LEVEL? WITH THE HELP OF NGOS

These developments are providing the basis for precisely the kinds of collaboration among NGOs that has been lacking in the past. Another aspect of this type of NGO networking is a more collaborative approach to working with governmental bodies, and a corresponding recognition by these bodies of how much they need NGOs. The North–South Centre, the European center for Global Interdependence and Solidarity, established by the Council of Europe, exists precisely to further interactive interdependence around the world. The July 1999 issue of its monthly newsletter, *The Interdependent,* offers a new publication, *NGO Guide 1999, Practical Information for NGOs within the European Union.* This detailed guide to NGO networks will be followed by a similar guide to the government-supported institutes and programs of the European Union. The same issue announces a new database for experience-sharing among NGOs engaged in similar projects, *Dialogue for Human Progress*, launched in 1998 by the Charles Leopold Mayer Foundation. The database already contains 7,000 "experience cards" from groups in 25 countries on four continents; each card a practical account of specific types of development actions. The North–South Centre's Newsletter is itself an action gold mine.[6]

Peace activists who have persisted in their activism through the ups and downs of 20th century wars understandably have come to think of governments as "the problem," yet it is important to remember that states have been struggling, especially since World War II, to find a way out of the mutually assured destruction trap created by the adoption of nuclear defense security policies by the major powers. In spite of official defense policies, an impressive number of high-ranking officials can be cited arguing for nuclear abolition in each of the nuclear weapons states. We must remember that a certain number of peace and justice activists with

[5]See Reconciliation International, magazine of the International Fellowship of Reconciliation, August 1999 issue, devoted to peace teams and nonviolence training (Spoorstraat 38, 1815 BK Alkmaar, The Netherlands).

[6]*The Interdependent* is available from the North–South Centre, Avenida da Liberdade 229–4, P 1250–142, Lisbon, Portugal.

international experience actually find their way into government posts in their respective countries (the Greens in Germany are a notable example) and also into the UN secretariat. They become a moderating influence and a communication channel with civil society that helps soften the resistance to change so notable in government policy.

Regarding denuclearization efforts alone, many thousands of person-hours of government representatives and diplomats have gone into each of the 33 agreements to limit nuclear and other types of weapons that have been signed between 1959 and 1996. Every agreement represents, however weakly, a process in which enough listening took place that a step forward in arms control was achieved, at least by the states signatory to the agreement. (Also, think of the thousands of person-hours spent by representatives of concerned NGOs in dialogue with government experts!) There is, after all, an incipient peace culture in the international community of diplomats that works to modify aggressive military strategies, a culture to be worked with by peace activist NGOs.

The strongest peace culture at the state level is to be found among the middle powers. Canada took the lead in getting the Landmine Treaty signed, and Australia convened the 1995 Canberra Commission on the Elimination of Nuclear Weapons that led to public support by 61 former generals and admirals and over a hundred public leaders for complete nuclear disarmament. Norway led the initiative to limit global small arms production and transfer. NGO activists in support of state initiatives played an important role in each of these cases and even more so in supporting state initiatives to establish regional nuclear weapon-free zones over the opposition of the nuclear powers. The Treaty of Tlatelolco (Latin America 1967), the Treaty of Raratonga (South Pacific 1985), the Bangkok Treaty (Southeast Asia 1995), and the Africa-wide Pelindaba Treaty, 1996, are all specifically stated by the signatory states as first steps toward complete disarmament (Alves and Cipollone, 1997). Preparations for a Central Asia nuclear weapon-free zone began at Almaty in 1997, making this a fifth zone, and a central European nuclear-free corridor is on the drawing board. In short, much of the world has declared itself nuclear free, in spite of the nuclear powers. None of these treaties would have come about without extensive NGO groundwork, nor would the 23 small states that have unilaterally declared themselves nuclear free have been able to do so without strong civil society support in each state.

One of the major obstacles to a strengthened peace culture within the existing state system is that the system itself is crumbling, as the ethnically, linguistically, or religiously based identity groups of the "10,000 societies" that are sprawled across all state boundaries vociferously assert their identity. Modernization theory assumed that each state would gradually assimilate all identity groups within its borders, yet the opposite is happening (including in the United States, which is supposed to be the great melting pot). Supposedly disappearing ethnies are reasserting themselves. This is a consequence of the failure of modern states to meet the needs of their diverse populations. Minorities are frequently economically disadvantaged (others are disproportionately advantaged) both in the West and in the Two-Thirds World. Many of the 137 states that joined the UN since 1945 are having highly conflictual internal power transitions. These struggles are directly traceable to two to four centuries of occupation by European colonizers, giving preferential treatment to some ethnies over others and creating inequalities and resentments that continue to fuel present-day conflicts. Nor are the founding states of the UN exempt from the problem. A survey I undertook in the 1970s revealed that only four countries out of the total UN membership at that time were monocultural; three of these were European, one Asian (Boulding, 1979). The intense and continuing efforts to evolve new constitutional formats in countries with strong communal groups, like Canada, Switzerland, Belgium, Spain, and the United Kingdom, are suggestive of new forms of local autonomy that will continue to arise, in some cases peacefully, in other cases very painfully. The Council of Europe encourages the recognition of autonomous regions within the states of its membership and provides for recognition of such regions, ethnies, and minority languages. The Organization of African Unity is trying to move in the same direction.

Ethnies should not be romanticized, but they need to be realistically recognized. Only since 1993, the UN International Year of Indigenous People, have indigenous peoples been counted as entities, let alone recognized as peoples. A peace culture at the level of the state system will certainly have to involve a new quality of relationships among ethnies within states based on respect, economic justice, and a recognition that each ethnie has valuable local knowledge and traditions, including conflict resolution skills, which can contribute to the larger polity.

THE UN: AN INTERSTATE CULTURE OF PEACE?

The UN itself, the body that somehow holds together its highly diverse 188 states, has to deal both with demands by ethnies for recognition and with the often uncompromising stances of the major powers in relation to national security, arms control, and disarmament. (Those powers often hold the Security Council hostage.) The UN is also the organization that benefits the most from the energy and know-how offered by relevant NGOs to its six major operating organs, 13 associated bodies, 16 specialized agencies, five regional commissions, fluctuating numbers of peacekeeping and observer missions (27 in 1998)—plus 20 research institutes, divisions, and special programs, and two UN-related universities. None of these could function without NGO support, a support that is of special relevance to the 188 UN Centers, one in each member state, which are the local UN face for that country. Operating with a minuscule budget and suffering from many bureaucratic deficiencies, the UN nevertheless somehow functions and offers a tantalizing glimpse of what an interstate culture of peace could be. My own experience of serving on the UN University Council, various UNESCO committees, working with several UN research institutes, and participating in a variety of peace and disarmament consultations at UN headquarters, has given me the greatest respect for the quality of the international civil servants who keep the UN functioning against heavy odds, decade after decade. Many readers will have had similar experiences.

The international communities of scholars who work with the UN University and the UN research institutes, such as UNIDIR, the UN Institute for Disarmament Research, and UNESCO's many peace-related programs, represent a significant partnership between the scholarly and scientific sectors of the global civil society, and the UN system itself, in the development of peace culture for the next century.

One particularly important UN–NGO interface is found in the UN peacekeeping missions, the Blue Helmets. Although originally seen as a resource for the international community to halt military conflict and bring warring parties to the table for diplomatic solutions, the necessary special training for UN soldiers in the minimization of violence and in skills of peacekeeping and peacebuilding has been very slow to develop. All too often, peacekeepers come to be seen as one more party to armed struggle. Observer missions, more likely to have special training, are somewhat more successful, and a serious review of UN peacekeeping training is now under way. The role of those NGOs with special expertise in conflict resolution and mediation has been enhanced by the recent emphasis on collaboration both at headquarters and in the field between the UN Department of Peacekeeping and the UN Department of Humanitarian Affairs. The latter regularly recruits people with humanitarian and peacebuilding expertise from the NGO community, and eventually NGO peace brigades may be able to work in cooperation with UN peacekeepers wherever the latter are stationed.

TRUTH AND RECONCILIATION

One overwhelming problem faced by every state is how to deal with the aftermath of violence and war, whether intrastate or between states. War is supposed to be fought between the soldiers of opposing armies, and civilians are supposed to be protected; so are food-bearing lands and orchards, in edicts laid down long ago in the Hebrew Bible, the Koran, and other sacred writings. The reality is that civilians and agricultural lands have never been safe. Rules about just war are periodically rewritten. Nevertheless, the protection of civilians remains at the core of such rules. After World War II, East German lawmakers eventually apologized for the Holocaust after their government had denied responsibility for decades. Japanese Prime Minister Tomiichi Murasama apologized for suffering inflicted in World War II. There has been much grieving over allied bombings over Europe but no formal apologies.

And what about the United States, the country that introduced nuclear bombs as a weapon of warfare in Japan? Although the government has made restitution to the Japanese–American families it arbitrarily interned during the war with Japan, the United States has never dealt with the reality of Hiroshima and Nagasaki and the massive civilian deaths caused by the bombing. All information about the fate of the citizens of Hiroshima and Nagasaki became classified material, and much of it remains classified today. Instead of dealing with guilt, the U.S. government rationalized the bombing as having speeded the ending of the war and, therefore, being a justified and useful act. (There is actually much evidence that the Japanese had already taken the first steps toward capitulation, as the recently published *Hiroshima's Shadow*, Bird and Lifshutz, 1998, makes clear.) The government's rationalization has remained so politically powerful that a recent effort to hold an exhibit at the Smithsonian Institute in Washington, DC, giving more details of what actually happened, was simply stopped by governmental pressure. Instead, the United States is now engaged in encouraging Japan to revive its earlier military traditions that the United States itself once intended to stamp out by means of a Peace Constitution imposed on Japan by the Occupation authorities. Now, "military necessity" requires that the Japanese become fully armed allies of the United States in an increasingly troubled region of Asia.

This failure to grieve on the part of the United States over its terrible devastation of Japanese cities (even while Allies and Germans alike in Europe grieved over the bombings of Dresden, London, and other European cities) has meant that Americans have never fully faced the horrors of modern warfare. More seriously, the United States has never taken responsibility for having introduced *nuclear* warfare into the world and still unrepentantly holds to a first-use-if-necessary doctrine. General George Lee Butler, who became Commander-in-Chief of the U.S. Strategic Command in 1991, responsible for the targeting of nuclear weapons against 12,500 targets in the Soviet Union, has spoken unequivocally of his horror when he became aware of the "defense" system that could exterminate 250 million Soviets, and possibly mankind in its entirety. He did his best to downgrade the system but finds now in his retirement that there is a creeping re-rationalization of nuclear weapons in the U.S. security community. An aroused American citizenry could never have allowed this to happen. But because there never was a national process of grieving over harm done in Japan, military policy has evolved without serious public objection. Peace movements have grieved, faith communities have grieved, but the general public has never grieved. Americans have never officially said they are sorry! This has profound implications for the United States' role in global peacekeeping as we enter a new millennium. "Bombing works" is the received wisdom on dealing with enemies; so the United States bombs Iraq daily even at this writing, and it bombed Serbia daily as long as the allies would let it. It is now enthusiastically building up its air force bombing capacity for the next decade. This sublimely self-assured military barbarism would appear to doom any possible spread of peace culture in the foreseeable future.

But something entirely different is happening in many of the countries that have been at war in recent decades. On the one hand, there has been the establishment of international tribunals to use the rule of law rather than force in judging acts of atrocity, a practice reaching from the Nuremberg and Tokyo Trials after World War II to the International Criminal Tribunals for the former Yugoslavia and Rwanda in the 1990s. Although legal judgment is often seen as inadequate in the face of great atrocities, a certain aura of fairness and accountability is established that, at the least, mutes the passions of the postwar situation.

Another related and more positive development has been the establishment of truth commissions, growing from the realization that cycles of vengeance and counter-vengeance can completely destroy the societies involved and must be stopped. There is a space, somewhere, to be reached between vengeance and forgiveness, where enemies can live together again. Whether the conflicting parties are tribal, clan-based, different ethnies, faith communities, or primarily political groupings, when the fighting stops, the parties must give each other room to get on with their lives. Because there has been much suffering, and usually all sides have experienced some injury, feelings of anger, hatred, and the desire for compensation are strong. Out of the urgent need to deal fairly with these feelings, governments, faith communities, and NGOs have worked together to develop a new type of institution for the modern world (and yet one that is often found in tribal and traditional "folk law")—the truth commission.

Turning from trials, which are slow and stress punishment, to truth commissions means settling for "all the truth and as much justice as possible." Yet truth and justice are not the only social needs to be met for societies to heal. Minow (1998) developed a list of twelve overlapping aspirations for such commissions:

1. Overcome communal and official denial of the atrocity and gain public acknowledgment.
2. Obtain the facts in an account as full as possible to meet victims' need to know, to build a record for history, and to ensure minimal accountability and visibility of perpetrators.
3. End and prevent violence; transform human activity from violence—and violent responses to violence—into words and institutional practices of equal respect and dignity.
4. Forge the basis for a domestic democratic order that respects and enforces human rights.
5. Support the legitimacy and stability of the new regime proceeding after the atrocity.
6. Promote reconciliation across social divisions; reconstruct the moral and social systems devastated by violence.

7. Promote psychological healing for individuals, groups, victims, bystanders, and offenders.
8. Restore dignity to victims.
9. Punish, exclude, shame, and diminish offenders for their offenses.
10. Express and seek to achieve the aspiration that "never again" shall such collective violence occur.
11. Build an international order to try to prevent and also to respond to aggression, torture, and atrocities.
12. Accomplish each of these goals in ways that are compatible with the other goals.

The South African Truth and Reconciliation Commission, which emphasizes amnesty and reconciliation while at the same time making room for prosecution of unrepentant offenders, is the best example we have of the positive potentials of what has come to be known as restorative justice. The fact that the commission was preceded for several years by the Peace Accord process, where national and local Accord groups worked to establish local dialogue and create mutual understanding among racial groups in the new post-apartheid South Africa, is sometimes overlooked. Although that process paved the way for the Truth and Reconciliation Commission, it in no way diminishes the latter's achievements. The commission process is long, slow, making many demands on the social energies of the society, but it is generally agreed that the process is "working." Other truth commissions put more emphasis on prosecution of atrocities, but positive potentials remain.

The 15 truth commissions reported by Neil Kritz in a recent U.S. Institute of Peace Study (Kritz, 1995) are tangible evidence of a new direction in dealing with the aftermath of war and violence. In the 1980s, Bolivia, Argentina, and Uruguay established national commissions on the Disappeared, and Uganda and the Philippines established commissions on violations of human rights. In the 1990s, Chile established a National Committee for Truth and Reconciliation, South Africa a Truth and Reconciliation Commission, Chad a Commission of Inquiry on Crimes, Rwanda a Commission on Human Rights Violations, El Salvador and Guatemala Truth Commissions, and Nicaragua a Law on General Amnesty and National Reconciliation. Brazil, Columbia, and Peru have all made efforts in the direction of truth commissions, with unclear outcomes. Germany established a Commission to Assess the History and Consequences of the East German Dictatorship. Truth commissions are sparse in Asia, although there have been initiatives in Sri Lanka, Cambodia, and elsewhere, and Japan has looked into the wartime abuse of Korean women as "comfort women." Running like a bright thread through all the commission and tribunal activities has been the effort to establish rape as a war crime, because the mass raping of women is one of the most widespread atrocities committed against civilians wherever there is violence of any kind.

Needless to say, all these efforts have been spurred by intense grass roots, NGO, and faith community activity in the countries in question, with outside support, as well. Bringing victims through grief is a very deep process, and much honor is due the many hundreds of volunteers who have worked to bring victims and victimizers, enemy and enemy together to listen to each others' stories and find a basis for moving forward together. Forgiveness and reconciliation are unrealistic goals in many situations, but some level of realistic acceptance of the need to work together can be and is often achieved.

Because women and children are the most frequent victims, and child soldiers as well as adults have been trained to torture and kill, the process of relearning one's humanity can be very difficult, indeed, both for the tortured and the torturers, and needs many trained helpers to facilitate the relearning. Reintegrating former guerillas and soldiers who have engaged in widespread torture is the challenge that has already led to a number of UNESCO culture of peace programs to carry out the healing. Local peace centers have played an important role, as well. Zoilamerica Narvaez has described this work in Nicaragua (Narvaez, 1997), where significant reintegration has taken place. Women play a special role as healers, as Narvaez exemplifies. She has many counterparts on every continent, perhaps most of all in Africa.

A little-known example of this type of healing work can also be found in the United States. A number of Vietnam Veterans have gone through a similar healing process, some of them under the tutelage of Thich Nat Hanh, who has traveled from France to the United States to conduct healing workshops under local Buddhist and local peace center auspices for those who seek them. In the speaking, listening, reflection, and the various practices developed for social healing for wounded societies lies hope for new images of the future, the possibility of strengthening human peaceableness, and channeling assertive energies into rebuilding human relationships for creative, adventurous tomorrows.

THE 200-YEAR PRESENT

It is hard to understand what is happening by only looking at the present moment. The concept of the 200-year present helps to open up the event space around us to get a different perspective on social process. The 200-year present begins with the birth 100 years ago of the centenarians who are celebrating their 100th birthday today; its other boundary is 100 years from today, when the babies born today will celebrate their 100th birthday. Although we will have lived only a part of this stretch of time, we will have had personal contact through family and friends with those born a century ago, and similarly, we will have personal contact with individuals who will be alive a century from now. In this sense, the 200-year span can be thought of as our own life space and helps us experience the immediacy of that which takes place in it. This brings all the developments of ethnies, states, the League of Nations and the UN, and the grass-roots and NGO groupings of the civil society—1899 to 2000—into our immediate present. It brings their continuing unfolding from 2000 to 2100 into our present as well. It is all *happening* in an extended *now.*

The grounds for hope for the next half of this extended present are that so much inventive peace culture has evolved over this period. As Kenneth Boulding used to say, "what exists is possible." The fact that so many peaceful ways of managing difference at every level from local to global have actually come into being means that it is possible for these peaceful ways to grow and expand, transforming the energies that have gone into violence and warfare into creative new social institutions and human activities.

Let us return to the concept of the role of positive images of the future in empowering action in the present. We have the challenge to imagine the further evolution of attitudes, values, behaviors, and institutional patterns that can sustain creativity, peaceableness, and human caring. This imagining is called on as humankind faces the problems of a heavily armed planet with nuclear and other weapon residues lurking on each continent, a planet with growing resource shortages, exhausted soils, water scarcity, and possible long-term climate change for populations that have grown beyond the carrying capacity of that planet. If we fail in our imagining capacity, the future looks dim indeed.

We have a decade now at hand where all the positive initiatives described in this article, by GROs, NGOs, ethnies, governments, interstate groups, and the UN itself, can be intensified through a process of mutual awareness among these highly diverse actors and a deliberate openness to experimentation and new social learnings about how to collaborate so the various betterment efforts enhance rather than diminish one another. The Internet, which tends to create information overload, will have a limited but important role. Most important will be face-to-face interaction across all the boundaries that complex social organizations generate. Solutions to the many problems we face do not lie in cyberspace but in the human heart, the listening ear, and the helping hand.

For starters, in the coming decade of education for a culture of peace and nonviolence, there could be a focus on local schoolrooms around the world, where teachers and community groups would develop school–community projects to bring children face to face with the peacemakers where they live—elders, local councils, healers, leaders in local faith groups, leaders in local market associations, women's organizations, and other grass-roots groups. In short, people in the local community can become visible to children, persons who can offer diverse models of nonviolent conflict resolution, including traditional practices that modernization has ignored, and who can share various local and cultural resources for peaceful ways of living. This would certainly include local musicians, singers, dancers, and artists. Once children understand local processes and resources, they can be introduced to the political and civic structures of their country responsible for the peaceful resolution of conflicts—as well as for human rights, economic development, stewardship of the environment, and economic justice. During this process, they could be introduced to the NGOs that bind their community to the global civil society. In this way, the current generation of the world's children can be prepared to enter those networks and participate in the growing partnership between governments, the UN, and NGOs.

A current proposal[7] suggests bringing together a team of peace educators, researchers, and peacebuilding practitioners from different world regions to explore the development of a curriculum guide, inclusive of learning experiences meaningful and relevant in the many geographic, ethnic, religious, and cultural settings to be found within the borders of the member states of the UN. Such a guide would be intended for local teachers and the local community organizations that would work with them. The inspiration for this project comes from the International Federation of Red Cross/Red Crescent Societies which has already developed a course for sixth-graders living in regions of violent conflict and war, to teach them about human rights and the laws of war, preparing them for their own possible future roles as soldiers—a practical way to help children understand that soldiers have a responsibility to protect civilians in wartime.

On the one hand, children could be prepared in their local schools and communities to become peacemakers. On the other hand, at the interstate level, the non-nuclear powers could be developing an increasingly strong coalition at the UN to bring about complete nuclear disarmament. Draft treaties have already been prepared to bring the remaining regions that have not already declared themselves to be nuclear weapons-free zones to become so. The Abolition 2000 NGO coalition will continue to grow in strength and play an important role in this process. The nuclear power states will not agree to this process at first, but over time, given resource shortages of every kind, generated by persistent droughts and environmental deterioration, the nuclear states may finally agree that they can no longer afford nuclear weapons. This outcome would be helped by the formation of strong national commissions in each nuclear power state giving voice to the widespread popular desire to end the threat of nuclear war and downsize the military generally. Such commissions will point out that national resources going to the military will be needed to meet more pressing social and environmental problems in states with aging populations. There has already been ample evidence of this military preference for military downsizing on the part of citizens in the closing decade of the 20th century (Kay, 1998).

---

[7]This initiative is in its early stages. A proposal has been sent out by Elise Boulding and Cynthia Cohen, Coexistence Program Director, from the International Center for Ethics, Justice, & Public Life at Brandeis University, Waltham, MA. Meanwhile, a local group of elementary school educators in New England is developing a curriculum for local use on "Making Peace Where I Live," hoping other groups will try similar projects based on local resources.

The leadership exercised by the middle powers in nuclear abolition will also reduce the power of the Security Council to the point where major reforms become possible in the UN itself, including the development of an expanded Security Council with more limited powers, and an NGO Assembly and a Peoples' Assembly to supplement the existing General Assembly. There could be a name change to something like the United Nations and Peoples Organization.

The collaboration among global and civil society bodies in these changes may be helped by an increasing practice of joint imaging workshops, in which participants step several decades into the future to imagine how things would look in a nuclear-free, life-friendly environment. After exploring this imagined terrain, participants then in imagination work their way back to the present, visualizing the kinds of events, activities, and changes in consciousness that might bring about such a future. These workshops, like workshops held in the closing decades of the 20th century, would end with specific commitments to action in the present to bring about the desired peaceful future.[8]

The key to this more promising second half of our 200-year present lies in our social imagination. It also lies in our willingness to look unflinchingly at both the potentials for and the obstacles to peace, and then move beyond the existing situation to build in a practical way on inclusive, creative mutual learning partnerships among the grass-roots groups, NGOs, ethnies, states, and interstate bodies that our wonderful difficult 20th century has produced. Such partnerships already exist and have produced good things. What exists is possible.

REFERENCES

Adams, D. (Ed.). (1991). *The Seville Statement on Violence, preparing the ground for the construction of peace.* Paris: UNESCO.

Alves, P. G., & Cipollone, D. B. (Eds.). (1997). *Nuclear-weapon-free zones in the 21st century.* Geneva, Switzerland: UN Institute for Disarmament Research.

Bird, K., & Lifshutz, L. (Eds.). (1998). *Hiroshima's shadow, writings on the denial of history and the Smithsonian controversy.* Stony Creek, CT: The Pamphleteer's Press.

Bonta, B. (1993). *Peaceful peoples: An annotated bibliography.* Metuchen, NJ: The Scarecrow Press.

Boulding, E. (1979). "Ethnic Separatism and World Development." In L. Kriesberg (Ed.), *Research in social movements, conflict and change,* Vol. 2. Greenwhich, CT: JAI Press.

Boulding, E. (1992). *The Underside of history: A view of women through time.* 2 vols. (Rev. ed.). Newbury Park, CA: Sage.

Boulding, E. (2000). "New partnerships: Women and men," in Chapter 6, *Cultures of Peace: The Other Side of History.* In press: Syracuse, NY: Syracuse University Press.

[8]A format for conducting Imaging the Future workshops can be found in Elise Boulding's *Building a Global Civic Culture, Education for an Interdependent World.* Syracuse, NY: Syracuse University Press, 1988. Appendix 2, pp. 172–176.

Fellman, G. (1998). *Rambo and the Dalai Lama, the compulsion to win and its threat to human survival*. Albany: State University of New York Press.

Grun, B. (1975). *The timetables of history. A horizontal linkage of peoples and events*. (Based on Werner Stein, *Kulturfahrplan*, 1946.) New York: Simon and Schuster.

Kay, A. (1998). *Locating consensus for democracy, a ten-year U.S. experiment*. St. Augustine, FL: Americans Talk Issues.

Kelman, H. (1986). "Interactive Problem Solving: A Social-Psychological Approach to Conflict Resolution." In W. Klassen (Ed.), *Dialogue toward interfaith understanding* (pp. 193–237). Tantur/Jerusalem: Ecumenical Institute for Theological Research.

Kritz, N. (Ed.). (1995). *Transitional justice: How emerging democracies reckon with former regimes. General considerations,* Vol. 1. Washington, DC: U.S. Institute of Peace.

Mayor, F. (1996). In D. Adams (Ed.), *UNESCO and a culture of peace program: Promoting a global movement* (pp. 26–27). Paris: UNESCO Culture of Peace Program.

McCarthy R., & Sharp, G. (1997). *Nonviolent action: A research guide*. New York: Garland.

Minow, M. (1998). *Between vengeance and forgiveness, facing history after genocide and mass violence*. Boston: Beacon.

Narvaez, Z. (Ed.). (1997). *Promotores de paz, revista del programa de educacion y accion para La Paz*. Vol. 2, Numero 1, Febrero. Managua, Nicaragua: Centro de Estudios Internacionales.

Polak, F. (1961). *The image of the future, translated by E. Boulding*. 2 vols. New York: Dobbs Ferry. Also 1 vol. abridgement by E. Boulding (1972). San Francisco: Jossey-Bass/Elsevier.

Schama, S. (1996). Flaubert in the trenches; a review of *Birdsong* by Faulks. *The New Yorker, 72*, 96–99.

Sharp, G. (1973). *The politics of nonviolent action*. Boston: Porter Sargent.

There exists an obligation to pursue in good faith and bring to a conclusion negotiations leading to nuclear disarmament in all its aspects under strict and effective international control.

International Court of Justice, July 8, 1996

PEACE AND CONFLICT: JOURNAL OF PEACE PSYCHOLOGY, *6*(3), 217–221

Structural Asymmetries and Peace: Hope or Despair?

Cheryl de la Rey
Department of Psychology
University of Cape Town

This article suggests that where one is positioned in the current geopolitical system is likely to have an influence on whether one feels hope or despair. In this respect material asymmetry as a divisive influence is noted and it is argued that poverty reduction is a crucial component in defining a culture of peace. The need for sharing of resources as envisioned in the definition offered by Boulding is endorsed. Although the reduction of material asymmetry is seen as crucial, it is however, not seen as sufficient for the attainment of a peace culture. Redressing other power differentials such as gender is also viewed as crucial. The insights offered by Elise Boulding on the role of nongovernmental organizations are highlighted but the need to examine civil society more widely is also noted. In particular, the question of the meaning of citizenship is emphasized. In conclusion, the importance of developing a holistic, interdisciplinary approach that draws on cooperation and interdependence is affirmed and it is argued that there is sufficient reason for hope.

"The century started off so promisingly" proffers Elise Boulding at the very outset of a highly thought-provoking article. "For whom?" I wondered in response. Did the century start off promisingly from the point of view of many of those at the southern tip of Africa? In South Africa the turn of the century was marked by the Anglo–Boer War, a power struggle amongst a White minority to determine authority and control over a region with a Black majority population who did not enjoy rights of citizenship. With many people in concentration camps and labour service, I wonder whether there was a general feeling of promise. I raise these questions not to produce answers, but to draw attention to the relevance of positionality.

Requests for reprints should be sent to Cheryl de la Rey, Department of Psychology, University of Cape Town, Private Bag, Rondebosch 7701, Cape Town, South Africa. E-mail: cdlr@psipsy.uct.ac.za

THE RELEVANCE OF POSITIONALITY

Where one is positioned in the global geopolitical system matters—it may determine whether one sees a problem or not and, if so, how the problem is defined and then, the solutions that are offered in response. Contemporary global geopolitics is shaped by inequalities at multiple levels and as Elise Boulding points out, some disparities seem to be increasing unchecked to the extent that "The rich grow richer, the poor grow poorer" (p. 198). Stark inequalities differentiate rich and poor, powerful and powerless. As we face the turn of another century, some people may feel hope and others may feel despair, depending on where they are positioned in relation to the disparities that divide human communities across the globe.

MATERIAL ASYMMETRY

Material asymmetry divides the nations of the world. Countries in Africa, South America, and Asia bear the burden of huge external debts and staggering levels of poverty. Economic inequities however, do not only divide north and south, industrialized and developing nations; material disparities also divide people within nations. Schwebel (1997), for example, drew attention to how people in the United States are divided by differential access to employment and job security. In pointing to the role of long-term unemployment, job insecurity, and underemployment in producing forms of contemporary violence, Schwebel was of course building on the work of Galtung (1996), who examined how inequities in economic systems constitute a form of structural violence that underlies the varied forms of violence and conflict that confront us as we enter the next century.

Poverty reduction is therefore a necessary and vital element in the work of those who seek to bring about peace in the world. Indeed, it is a crucial component of Elise Boulding's working definition of peace culture. Sharing resources is integral to her definition. Rightly so, as the sharing of resources is a challenge that confronts us all at several levels. First, at the global level there are several pressing issues around foreign aid, the cancellation of debt, and equitable trade. Second, at the regional level there are a number of agreements that attempt to reduce disparities through economic and political cooperation. In southern Africa the agreements and ongoing dialogue among the countries that form the Southern Africa Development Community are examples. Third, at the national level the challenge to achieve a more equitable distribution of wealth among citizens is an issue for nearly all countries, from those among the wealthiest such as the United States (as pointed out by Schwebel, 1997), to those countries that rank among the poorest. It is the most pressing challenge for South Africa, my native country. Job creation, the provision of housing, education, and health and social services to the poor are among the key issues to be dealt with by South Africa's second democratically elected government as this century gives way for the next.

POWER DIFFERENTIALS

But, even though redressing material inequalities is fundamental to the creation of a peace culture, it is not sufficient for, as many cases show, economic asymmetries are often inextricably interwoven into other systems of powerlessness and oppression. The absence of power differentials is therefore a necessary and important component of Elise Boulding's working definition of a peace culture. Again, she rightly points out that a culture of peace involves nurturant living and this cannot occur where there are structured power differentials.

Gender

Gender as a locus of power difference is often not given sufficient attention in our analyses of major social issues. Gender-based violence such as rape, sexual harassment, and domestic abuse is one of the most widespread forms of violence that occur during times of war, in the aftermath, and during times when there is no ostensible warfare. It is a pervasive form of violence. I believe that given the enormity of the problem more space may have been given to a more probing analysis of gender in the article. Gender is alluded to, but not in sufficient depth.

One of the gender-related ideas is that women have a special role in bringing about social transformation. Is this justified, I wonder? Although there is evidence that women are less likely than men to initiate and perpetrate violence, there is also evidence that women are just as likely as men to uphold, perpetuate, and collude in systems of oppression. Moreover, given that women as a group are underrepresented in governments and other institutions that wield power and authority, our potential to have an impact is likely to be rather limited at the global, regional, and national levels unless we form strong coalitions and mass-based movements. On this specific note, the article suggests that there is hope as civil society is flourishing as never before. In support of this the growing number of nongovernmental organizations (NGOs) across the world is noted.

THE ROLE OF NGOS

With reference to the role of NGOs, Elise Boulding offers several insightful comments. The positive contribution made by NGOs in raising awareness around key issues, in challenging dominant views and ways of knowing and in developing knowledge that is useful in working toward cultures of peace is foregrounded, yet constructive critique of NGOs is also offered. The article points to their tendency toward parochialism, territorialism, and sometimes insensitivity toward local, contextual needs. Nonetheless, there is no doubt that NGOs are important and perhaps this is especially so with regard to gender issues. In South Africa the struggle for gender equality is currently most visible within the domain of NGOs that undertake activities such as lobbying, advocacy, education, and the provision of services such as counseling.

NGOs are undoubtedly an important presence in civil society. However, any tendency to simply equate civil society with the existence of NGOs must be avoided. There are numerous areas and individuals outside of the reach of NGOs; in many contexts these are likely to be individuals living in poor, rural areas at the margins of the structures and processes of organized civil society and government. What is the experience of civil society for such people?

THE MEANING OF CITIZENSHIP

Confronting the question of the meaning of citizenship is crucial to the building of peaceful societies. What we have learned from history is that the exclusion of people from citizenship leads to violence. For the majority of South Africans citizenship only became a lived reality in this last decade of the 20th century. Therefore, for us it is a precious and contested concept. The first experience of citizenship for most South Africans was lived through the act of voting in 1994. Six years later after having voted for the second time, there is an awareness that citizenship involves more than the act of voting; it includes participation and representation in the institutions of society. But, a pressing question yet to be dealt with satisfactorily, is how to ensure equal participation, representation, and rights for people who differ from one another in many respects—ethnicity, religion, gender, and culture are but a few of the sites of difference. Too frequently equality of citizenship is interpreted as sameness with the effect of disrespecting difference. The attainability of global peace depends on our ability to find workable solutions to these and other questions.

Developing the meaning of citizenship, finding ways to minimize asymmetries, and overcome structural violence fits in well with the general shift in peace-related work away from a narrow focus on violence and its consequences toward a greater focus on prevention and sustainability. It is vitally important that we continually examine the past to uncover the lessons to be learned from history so that we can prevent the mistakes of the past. In so doing we have to be careful not to overly focus on the conflicts of the past, but to also examine, as Elise Boulding does, the lessons to be learned from the places and times when peace has been enjoyed.

A Holistic Approach

To derive maximum gain from scrutinizing the past as well as probing new questions and challenges, we need a holistic interdisciplinary approach and the kind of collaborative reflection envisioned in the article. As pointed out, we lose numerous opportunities for developing new knowledge through duplication, turfism, and competitive efforts rather than collaboration and interdependence. Nevertheless, there is sufficient reason for hope—this is to be seen in the various millennialist peace efforts in the NGO sector as described in the article. But perhaps the greatest source of hope is to be found in a lesson gleaned from history, namely that change is inevitable and that movements to end oppression, violence, and war can bring about immense positive changes. In recent history South Africa is a case in point.

REFERENCES

Galtung, J. (1996). *Peace by peaceful means*. London: Sage.

Schwebel, M. (1997). Job insecurity as structural violence: Implications for destructive intergroup conflict. *Peace and Conflict: Journal of Peace Psychology*, *3*(4), 333–351.

Injustice, oppression, fraud, lying, whatever acts would be crimes, whatever habits would be vices if manifested in the pursuit of individual interests, when manifested in pursuit of national interests become sublimated into virtue.

Jeremy Bentham, 1789

PEACE AND CONFLICT: JOURNAL OF PEACE PSYCHOLOGY, *6*(3), 223–228

Can There Be Mutualism Among Humankind?

Caroline Lamwaka
The New Vision Corporation, Kampala, Uganda

"Mutualism" as opposed to "dominance" in both interpersonal and interstate relations is a grand vision, which could offer hope to many people as the path toward a more peaceful global environment. But can all humankind embrace the spirit of mutualism? Humans have tended to glamorise warfare in many parts of the world. For instance, those who have captured state power through guerrilla warfare have tended to over-glamorise their achievements, sending the wrong signal to the young people that "the gun is mightier."

In Africa, many people think that violence as a means of changing governments has been encouraged by the emergence of these guerrilla wars, many of which have managed to achieve their major goals and objectives—at least in the short run. Nongovernmental organisations (NGOs) and other pressure groups may offer better ways of building a peace culture when they preach nonviolence, reconciliation, and forgiveness. But NGOs have their limitations.

The emergence of intrastate and interstate wars has been one of the greatest challenges of the 20th century. As Elise Boulding in her article, "*A New Chance for Human Peaceableness?*" pointed out, the 20th century started off so promisingly. Could it be that the people of the world had embraced the 20th century with the same "millennial optimism" as that now being created among nongovernmental organisations (NGOs) within the global civil society today with the arrival of the "magic" year 2000? This would mean then that global peace is a Utopian affair for which we can only dream.

But "mutualism" as opposed to "dominance" in both interpersonal and interstate relations is not just Utopian. It is a grand vision, which could offer hope to many people as the path toward a more peaceful global environment. Hope is the

Requests for reprints should be sent to Caroline Lamwaka, c/o The New Vision Corporation, P.O. Box 9815, Kampala, Uganda. E-mail: vision@imul.com

source of our strength to continue with our positive plans from day to day for survival and for prosperity. However, can there be a paradigm shift from dominance to mutualism? Is it possible to build a culture of peace and nonviolence that would lead to human peaceableness?

This article wishes to point out that mutualism—possibly the best catch phrase for any peace worker—will most likely not be embraced by all humankind. The chain of mutualism may be embraced for a short time, say for only 10 years, only to be interrupted by violence in between. This is because one of humankind's basic instincts is the will to dominate, to conquer, to assert one's self, or to prosper over others. As a result, the world has continued to have "islands of peace" and "zones of insecurity." In the real world, the weak and vulnerable ones are taken advantage of as opposed to close collaboration for mutual gains.

Conflicts arise due to a number of factors, out of which violence may erupt. Violence may then become the means for self-defense, political domination or influence, or a way to exploit, steal, or loot resources from others.

Thus building a culture of nonviolence may not necessarily lead to human peaceableness unless political problems are consistently addressed at both the national and international levels.

THE UGANDAN EXPERIENCE

The wars experienced in Uganda have been mainly soldier-to-soldier rather than between members of the civil society. The nature of violence, with the exception of the Karimojong cattle raiders in northeastern Uganda, has often been such that violence started from the top as a means of solving a political problem, and then it percolated into the society.

The first real bloodbath in independent Uganda, after more than 60 years of colonial rule, took place in 1966, after independence in October 1962. It was a conflict between the then Executive Prime Minister, Milton Obote, and the ceremonial President, Sir Edward Mutesa, who was also King of Buganda, one of several kingdoms in Uganda.

The conflict between the Prime Minister and the President was about who was more powerful. Meanwhile, Sir Edward Mutesa had the conflicting role of being both President of a country and King of an ethnic group within a multiethnic society. The conflict turned partly on who controlled the economic surplus in Buganda, where the seat of government also lay.

Meanwhile there was also infighting within the ruling Uganda People's Congress party, with the anti-Obote faction competing for political power with Obote, allegedly backed by Sir Edward Mutesa. (Mutibwa, 1992, p. 37). On February 22, 1966, Obote took over the powers of government "in the interest of national unity and public security and tranquillity" (Mutibwa, 1992, p. 39). Two days later, he suspended the 1962 Independence Constitution and abolished the post of President. The Buganda Parliament passed a resolution calling on the Central Government to remove itself from Buganda's soil, a move that led to "the battle of Mengo" of May 1966 when the Central Government troops attacked the King's palace. Mutesa escaped to England.

When Idi Amin took over power from Obote in a military coup on January 25, 1971, he took the opportunity to eliminate his enemies, who happened to be from the ethnic groups, that dominated the security forces. He then went on to victimise other prominent members of the Ugandan civil society. On April 11, 1979, a joint force of the Tanzanian Army and Ugandan liberators ousted Amin.

Hopes were high that the move would usher in a new era of peace. But alas, although the Ugandan liberators had organised themselves politically under an umbrella organisation, Uganda National Liberation Front, there was still factional infighting for power. A president was installed and removed within 68 days, whereas his immediate replacement ruled for only slightly over a year after which a Military Commission took over and proceeded to oversee the electoral process of December 1980.

The elections turned out to be a disaster in the sense that the leader of one of the four contesting parties, Yoweri Museveni, went to the bush to fight a guerrilla war on grounds that the elections had been rigged. Obote was returned to power for the second time. Meanwhile, the bush war launched by Museveni in Luwero, north of Buganda, caused much suffering to the people there and the then Uganda government army, Uganda National Liberation Army, was accused of large-scale atrocities in the area.

As the war became more biting, a faction of Obote's army overthrew him on July 27, 1985, amidst complaints. General Tito Okello, who became President for 6 months, called on all groups who had been fighting Obote's government to come out and join hands with his government. All came out except Museveni's National Resistance Army/Movement (NRA/M). Peace talks were held in Nairobi, Kenya, between Museveni's and Tito Okello's groups, but the peace accord was never adhered to as the NRA/M broke the cease-fire and fought to capture power on January 26, 1986.

The current war in northern Uganda, which began in August 1986, is a continuation of that sad part of our history. My researches on the civil war in Uganda has revealed that mistrust, suspicion, hatred, and revenge have been the major cause of the war, especially among the soldiers. Both the government and the rebels have since committed large-scale atrocities in the course of fighting. Many people have died as a direct consequence of the violence itself. Others, mainly children, have suffered abductions, torture, or mistreatment at the hands of rebels in the bush. They are trained to fight and to kill. Families have been caught up in the middle of the war and are, at the time of this writing, still living in designated camp areas, officially known as "protected villages."

In the camps, many people, especially children and the elderly, have died due to the prevalence of war and sanitation-related illnesses like measles, malnutrition, tuberculosis, malaria, respiratory tract infection, eye infection, and bloody diarrhea, among others. To this category of people, life has lost its full meaning. This is where NGOs and international aid agencies like the International Committee of the Red Cross and the United Nations' World Food Program have come in to help create an atmosphere of peace. They have helped make the people realise that life can become better again.

We have seen our societies degenerate overnight from the 1970s to date. Society has so glamorised wars as something heroic to the extent that the young generation in Uganda is being politically re-educated and introduced to violence as a method of self-defense by the government. Yet the same program could still be abused, and the people trained could be used to fight wars even against their own will. For instance, since 1994 and as of the time of this writing, Uganda has been involved in war with the Sudan and from 1998 it has had troops stationed in the Democratic Republic of Congo.

In Africa, those who have captured state power through guerrilla warfare have tended to over-glamorise their achievements, sending the wrong signal to the young people that "the gun is mightier." For example, in the 1980s came the "revolutionary period" where governments considered dictatorial in Uganda, Ethiopia, Eritrea, and Somalia, among others, were overthrown by force of arms. Already from the 1950s there had been several guerrilla wars in South Africa, Angola, Mozambique, and Namibia, as a means of attaining independence from White rule. Many people think that violence as a means of changing governments in Africa has been encouraged by the emergence of these guerrilla wars, many of which have managed to achieve their major goals and objectives—at least in the short run.

The Vikings, the Greek, and other warrior societies may have dreamed of the joys of peaceful lifeways, where former enemies walked hand in hand, but perhaps because they were already war weary, and the wars impacted negatively on them. Or perhaps they too felt that they were fighting wars that would take them nowhere.

CAN NGOs DELIVER?

NGOs and other pressure groups may offer better ways of building a peace culture when they preach nonviolence, reconciliation, and forgiveness in a timely manner, while helping contribute to the development of a country.

In northern Uganda, some NGOs, as part of their healing work, are preaching forgiveness and reconciliation to the children and adults formerly abducted by rebels. They are reintegrating them into the societies. Here NGOs have been useful in sensitizing the society on how to receive the formerly abducted children so that the society sees that it was no fault of the children that they were trained to kill. The children are immediately accepted back into the society.

But NGOs have their limitations. What NGOs and other members of the civil society have built over a long period of time have often been destroyed overnight through violence or political turmoil. Most NGOs do not have the capacity to prevent wars that may erupt from a political crisis because they do not have the leverage to stop belligerent parties from fighting for what they consider dear to their hearts.

NGOs operating in a country do so under the supervision of the governments in power and many tend to bend to the wishes of those governments. To a large extent, their neutrality is compromised, as they have to work supporting the governments in power. For instance, as Elise Boulding has indicated in her article, the fact that bureaucratic shortcuts and compromises with representatives of the major powers resulted in the failure of the Hague Assembly 1999 to condemn the NATO bombing that was going on in Yugoslavia clearly shows the failure of NGOs. Most NGOs owe their existence to the governments in power and are not capable of condemning anything that puts them in an unfavourable position with the governments. In some countries in Africa, if you do undertake such actions, you may not get a certificate for registration, or your certificate could be withdrawn.

International NGOs based abroad may be neutral, but will still lack the effectiveness they would have if they were based within a particular country of operation. NGOs also largely operate on their own and not as a group. They are competitive, farther apart, and lack the capacity to come out as one front. They also do not have resources of their own and are largely dependent on donations from governments or the donor communities. Thus, they are weak in putting pressures on governments unlike, for instance, a superpower mediator like the United States, which can provide resources or loans, or commit the IMF or the World Bank to provide credit to governments as a means of getting them to talk to their opponents.

NGOs are indeed the closest to the civil society as they pursue humanitarian, cultural, scientific, and other concerns independent of governments. But many NGOs seem comfortable enough doing humanitarian work without addressing the root causes of the problems that create violence. They fear getting involved in issues that have serious political implications. They may build social institutions, but unless the political problems are addressed, it is most likely that some of those social institutions may crumble as problems they cannot cope with overwhelm them.

It is thus still unrealistic to bank our hopes on NGOs as the major foundation for human peaceableness.

CONCLUSION

More research is needed on the conditions of peace and the causes of war, as well as training in conflict resolution, mediation, and conflict transformation, in a bid to create as much as possible conditions that are peaceful in our environment. The establishment of a tribunal or truth commission is a very crucial step toward a healing process once war has stopped. The use of the rule of law rather than force in judging acts of atrocity is the only way forward in helping avert the possibility of further violence, and the only sure path toward reconciliation.

Governments must be willing to listen to advice from its citizens and NGOs. In Africa, overstay in power has been one of the main causes of violence as a means of changing governments. However, one of the biggest setbacks in developing countries has been lack of enough education among the majority of the population, which still renders them vulnerable to political manipulations. The civil society is still weak, disorganised, and lacks enlightenment. It needs empowerment through education and sensitization, and NGOs could effectively play their roles toward this goal.

REFERENCES

Mutibwa P. (1992). *Uganda since independence*. Kampala, Uganda: Fountain Publishers Ltd.

PEACE AND CONFLICT: JOURNAL OF PEACE PSYCHOLOGY, *6*(3), 229–235

The Future of Humanity: Human, Gender and Ecological Security

Ursula Oswald Spring
Regional Center of Multidisciplinary Research
National Autonomous University of Mexico
President, International Peace Research Association

In response to Elise Boulding's question whether there is a new chance for human peaceableness, this commentary starts by spelling out the four major problems left from the last century: poverty, violence, ecological destruction, and discrimination, especially against women, children, ethnic and minority groups, and the elderly. Then, against a brief historical background and following a description of a disillusioning experience at the Second Hague Conference in 1999, it charts a possible way to a culture of peace.

The dawn of the new millennium finds the world faced with profound contradictions. Four billion human beings live in material poverty, and humanity as a whole is trying to find new values and spiritual experiences that will allow it to live through this historical moment with less social and personal pain, but also, with more trust and security. The huge problems spilled over from the 20th century can be grouped into four great blocks: *poverty*; *violence,* including the armament industry and wars; *ecological destruction*; *discrimination* against women, children, ethnic and minority groups, and the elderly. Some resolution of any of these four sets of problems would introduce a process of change with positive effects on the other three, due to the fact that they are all interrelated.

Recognizing the enormous number of people affected by the aforementioned problems, it is urgent that we act in a different way from the past, because in the past not one of these problems has been resolved. The scientific and technological advances of the last 100 years offer us hope. These advances are such that there ex-

Requests for reprints should be sent to Ursula Oswald Spring, President, International Peace Research Association, Regional Center of Multidisciplinary Research, National Autonomous University of Mexico, Mexico. E-mail:uoswald@servidor.unam.mx

ists enough knowledge to feed all of humanity, guarantee a dignified and plentiful life, overcome violence and armed conflicts, and preserve the natural resources for coming generations. However, this knowledge, concentrated in the hands of interests alien to human and natural well-being, has been only partially used. These interests have promoted the arms race, which has increased violence, wars, and destruction never before known. Between 1990 and 1995, 70 states were involved in 93 wars, killing 5.5 million people, including 1 million children. Another frightening statistic is the worldwide 40 million refugees, the majority being women and children. As a result of recent conflicts, modern weapons cause immense environmental destruction that has life-threatening implications for all, but especially for women who are generally responsible for the well-being of their families, because of their reproductive role in which they often suffer the horrific consequences of biological and chemical warfare.[1] Severely deformed children, who, if they do not die at birth, or shortly after, require specialized help, which can be very difficult for poor women, who are forced to work or who live in refugee camps. Not only genetic defects, but also sterility and long-term degenerative health problems can be the outcome of a heavily polluted atmosphere due to war and the type of weapons and ammunition used (e.g. uranium bullets used by NATO during the ex-Yugoslavia's war in March 1999). We must conclude that the advances of science, which offer us hope, also have fallen far short of inducing social progress.

The globalization of the economy also did not induce social progress. On the contrary, it promoted a concentration of 45% of the world's wealth in the hands of five multinational enterprises (Cavagan, 1999). This forces 6 billion inhabitants of this planet to find some mechanisms of control and of achieving a more just distribution of that wealth. This is particularly important when we consider that four fifths of human beings live in poverty and miserable conditions, most of them women and children (UNICEF, 2000; World Bank, 1999). This condition of social polarization is not homogenous. It is concentrated in the Third World and recently also, the Second World. Women, children, the elderly, and ethnic minorities are the primary victims.

The problems of globalization present challenges never known before and if they are not resolved, they continue to represent a severe mortgage on the future, creating vulnerable conditions capable of affecting the stability of the planet. An explicit case was the recent monetary crisis of Mexico, Russia, Brazil, and Southeast Asia, which went beyond the specific economic parameters (money market, trade, banks, and stock market), and affected productivity, employment, income,

[1]In the Gynecological Obstetrician Hospital Tu Du in Saigon there are thousands of malformed fetuses in alcohol, as a result of spraying 76 million liters of herbicides over Vietnam between 1961 and 1972. Agent Orange contains TCDD, which is the most toxic dioxin and provokes severe diseases such as cancer, chlorine-acne, and hepatic disorders. More than 500,000 children born after 1960 are deformed due to dioxins (Warwick, 1999).

quality of life, and the survival of millions of human beings. But this also lessened the trust of the population in the banks, the government, and even the capitalist system, manifesting fragility never before imagined, especially in the case of the Japanese crisis, which affected the second largest economy of the world.

The globalization of the mass media of communication allows us to report almost instantly any catastrophic or bellicose event, even in the most remote parts of the planet. Its preference in violent and perverse contents at the same time that it stimulates consumerism and homogenization of Western culture destroys deep human values owned by all humanity, such as dignity, solidarity, and respect for life and nature. But it also erodes the internal peace of an individual, the values of the young people, and the belief in a better future.

In addition to the other social problems, the dramatic increase of natural disasters, some of them the result of the serious ecological imbalance, should alarm any human being. Ecological disasters have no respect for class, sex or age, and they become the most democratic process of destruction. Even though the infrastructure of civil protection in the poor countries is less advanced and thus the catastrophes cost more human lives, the mitigation requires, on a planetary scale, new forms of consumption, alternative management of mass media, and a new grass-roots participation stemming from awareness of the existing deterioration. However, some interests alien to the well-being of humankind, such as the powerful oil multinationals, place in checkmate even the survival of the earth, all on behalf of the maximization of individual benefits. Results such as global warming or depletion of the ozone layer go beyond local effects and threaten large parts of the globe.

HISTORY OPENS THE POSSIBILITY OF SOLUTIONS IN TWO DIRECTIONS

Elise Boulding's article clearly shows that the "war-making" story is written by the powerful, all of them men avid for power. But that is not intrinsic in the human being. From both a psychosocial and historical perspective, humans have the option of violence or pacific resolution of conflict. However, dominant forces tend to magnify the negative side and thereby provoke major contradictions in individuals. Her statement also shows that the globalization of capitalism within a framework of ferocious competition for markets and consumers either will solve the four major problems already mentioned, to generate conditions of sustainability for the future, or on the contrary, will lead the world down a blind alley of growing concentration of wealth, marginalization of majorities, and destruction of nature, where increasing violence threatens countless lives.

Her analytical exploration of the alternative movements, such as nongovernmental organizations (NGOs) and grass-roots organizations (GROs) suggests the possibility that they could crystallize the dreams of "joys of peaceful lifeways." Her article begins with a reflection on The First Hague Conference in 1899, where war was humanized (the foundation of the International Red Cross, The Treaties of War Prisoners, and those Injured in Battle), as well as the enforcement of the Westphalia Treaties, from 1848. The latter should have promoted respect for any nation–state, the negotiated resolution of controversy between sovereign states and the nonintervention of other nations in internal issues, premises that became the basic principles of the United Nations (UN). However, the hierarchical organization led by Czar Nicolas and the Queen of the Netherlands did not generate a framework of pacific resolutions of the existing conflicts, in the context of a Europe assaulted more and more by the economic and technological developments of the United States. The Russian Revolution occurred soon after, followed by two world wars, deep economic crisis, and the disintegration of European colonialism. Instead of consolidation and pacific resolution of conflicts, the bloodiest events of history occurred.

Violence, death, and exploitation followed its course during the whole century. At its end, the Second Hague Conference, The Hague Appeal 1999, organized by and for NGOs and GROs, appeared to lead the way toward an alternative and more hopeful future world. The organization model and the imposition of Western efficiency basically frustrated these hopes. Some of the factors which limited The Hague's range were the emphasis on numbers of participants, instead of quality of participants and contents; a scenario of spectacle instead of penetrating analysis; rhetoric instead of concrete actions; speaking instead of listening; plenaries dedicated to the parade of public personalities instead of proposals for alternative paradigms; a lack of common strategies for pacific conflict resolutions; the organization of a fully-packed but superficial program that hindered the elaboration of desirable future scenarios; discrimination against southern cultures and the imposition of English as official language without translation; the lack of space for workshops and encounters outside the program; no space to sit down, to talk, or simply relax; and expensive food with low nutritional quality. All of the aforementioned factors prevented the GROs and NGOs, the women and children, the people from the south, and the activists, from finalizing concrete actions, respectful of their cultural and geographical diverse contexts, but guided by an overarching framework. In summary, the experience was a faithful reflection of the dominant geopolitical forces whose individual interests, empty speeches, spectacle, apparent efficiency, westernized organization, led by male executives, predominated.

Despite this criticism, as a female participant, coming from the Third World, and working in the fields of peace, food, and ecology, I returned to Mexico with new utopias and a dream of a possible future, thanks to the discussions held among women where supportive men participated in this dream to create a new world. Even though the events related to gender issue were held simultaneously and therefore interfered with the establishment of networks and new ideas, the personal encounters with social activists opened new perspectives for the future. The supportive behavior of "women in black" of war-torn ex-Yugoslavia reinforced interethnic links, and did so as a courageous challenge in front of an authoritarian internal power (Milosevic) and another external one (NATO). The same could be said of the massive Japanese participation in opposition of any nuclear rehearsal or proliferation of atomic bombs. All these activities may awaken the sleepy North American society so that it demands from government and Congress a congruent response in accordance with the humanism, which it apparently propagates.

In a broader historical context, the social movements after World War II were against nuclear arms and war; against holocaust or any genocide; for a durable peace and nonviolent conflict resolution; for the struggle against colonialism; for a new international economic order for the Third World; and supportive of student, feminist, ecological, and anticonsumerism movements. All of these had and still have a common content: their objective—to guarantee security and a decent quality of life to the weakest. In a globalized world, every conflict has general repercussions and affects other areas. For this reason, the coordination of actions, where simultaneously the groups work on a planetary scale and in the microcommunity or microfamily in favor of peace, overcoming poverty, mitigation of environmental destruction, and integration of women, ethnic, religious, or cultural minorities, leads the way to hopeful perspectives for the 21st century.

The destruction of the socialist society by an authoritarian bureaucracy, and also the "end of history" (Fukutama, 1997), propagated by a neoliberal and transnational capitalism, force the vast majority of the world population to develop its own survival strategies (Oswald, 1990). The crude reality of discrimination and expulsion from the dominant model not only of the people from the South, but increasing numbers of people in the industrialized countries, opens new perspectives for solidarity and creativity about new societal directions. The increasing social gap, which exists in the midst of rhetoric about equality, but without equalizing social conditions and access to wealth, is the most important contradiction confronting us in this new century.

An array of dissimilar groups such as that of religious leaders, GROs, NGOs, and mothers, have organized against this gross inequality and against the daily violence. That violence has entered their homes and their classrooms and, primarily through the mass media, is having a profound influence on young people. Yet, whereas globalization discriminates and excludes, in a contradictory way, it also advances alternative communication media by opening new spaces of world solidarity through television and the Internet. These have a powerful bearing on processes of democratization and civil education in regions where authoritarian regimes previously prohibited the arrival of any news not belonging to their own ideology. Positive examples of pacific conflict resolution, the integration of different cultures, and of GROs that improve conditions of life, would help promote a less violent and fair and just world. This could convert citizens, but especially those "without voice," to become active protagonists for a better future. The decentralization and reinforcement of actions, enriched by the exchange of experiences and by world solidarity, as well as by clear knowledge that a consumer society does not guarantee quality of life, opens up the possibility of overcoming the severe world problems.

THE UTOPIA OF THE FUTURE

The integration of social, spiritual, environmental, feminist, and pacifist values all over the world could alter social and political action at the macro and micro levels, as recent protests against the World Trade Organization in Seattle in December 1999 demonstrate. The advancement of a democratic system, with the power of the ballot, in support of the genuine interests of the majorities, would force future politicians who want to be reelected to defend the interests of their constituents, even of the lowest social classes. At this time, some all-powerful multinationals can not only jeopardize weak states, but also the major powers due to their enormous and ever-increasing economic strength. This real danger forces all nations for the sake of stability and the common interest, to delimit the multinationals' excess of economic power and place it at everybody's service. Concrete mechanisms could be utility distribution, taxes (for instance, tax on speculative money), laws restricting monopolies, fair and just salaries and social welfare services, reduction of military expenses, and special contributions to those in need. The resultant resources would overcome extreme poverty and improve the environment. The policy changes would also guarantee a less violent future. Peace education could complement the economic actions, with courses, games, and other activities aimed at inculcating methods of nonviolent conflict resolution, from elementary school up to the university, and with couple and family therapy, and other psychological practices to help achieve internal peace.

Additionally, the negative experiences in both hemispheres question habits and cultural prejudices (ethnocentrism) belonging to the western countries: a better income is linked with less free time and less rest periods; major geographical mobility goes with the loss of human relations, social commitments, interfamilial relations, and communitarian links; work for wages substitutes subsistence family work, guided toward a productive life at a small scale and related self-consumerism; and success and social access limit the quality of interpersonal relations, produces phenomena of stress, and leaves less free time. For this reason the benefits of sustainable development combined with internal peace extend from the economy to health, life quality, and interpersonal relations. Globalization with such objectives would, in effect, integrate the slogans of different world conferences such as "little but beautiful"; "think globally, act locally"; "less consumerism, more life quality"; and "justice and peace for all."

Such a distinctive form of globalization, free of control by monopolies and multinationals, is yearned for in the northern countries, as an escape from dispersonalization, the illnesses of stress and the immune system, and poor quality of life, whereas it is yearned for in the south, which is harassed by extreme poverty, infrahuman life conditions, joblessness, deep inequality, and an increasing gap between social groups.

A globalization based on the solidarity of people would allow a new paradigm of nations and peoples living together, removed from the terror of arms, and personal psychical and social destruction. It would create an alternative concept of security. In this model, economic policy would be oriented to harmony between diverse segments of the society, and also between society and the environment. The economic policy would be based on knowledge and commitment achieved through consensus and respect for diversity.

This view of global sustainability is anchored in regional and local dynamics. It would benefit from the economy of scale and would support the most vulnerable groups. Although it would have world laws and norms, linked with surveillance and general sanctions (for instance, in the hands of a nonbureaucratized UN, but never of a superpower), its legitimacy would be based on the political, religious, and administrative organizations which would have emerged historically from each region. Its execution would also occur at the micro level in a way to overcome exacerbated nationalism and regionalism. It would reduce the fracture of political blocks, the disarticulation of nation–states, the dehomogenization of citizen behaviors, the religious and ideological fundamentalism, and separatist tendencies. A leitmotiv of the collective decision making would be that reflected by *Human, Gender and Ecological Security: HUGES* (Oswald, 2000). Such an approach would definitely go beyond the notion of equilibrium and security based on the terror of arms, the existence of one superpower, and NATO.

In conclusion, there is no greater challenge in this new century than to use civilization's enormous intellectual, scientific, and moral capacities to create a culture of peace that favors a decent life for all, and solidarity in the family, the community, and the world.

REFERENCES

Cavagan, J. (1999, May). *"Oral invervention about economic globalization,"*. Conference at The Hague Appeal.

Oswald, U. (1990). *Estrategias de superviviencia.* Cuernavaca, Mexico: UNAM/CRIM.

UNICEF (2000). *The state of childhood in the world* (El estado de la infancia en el mundo). New York: UNICEF–UN.

Warwick, H. (1998). *The Ecologist, 28*(5), 17–18.

World Bank (1999). *World development indicators.* Washington, DC: World Bank.

All social scientists, by the fact of their existence, are involved in the struggle between enlightenment and obscurantism.

C. Wright Mills, 1959

PEACE AND CONFLICT: JOURNAL OF PEACE PSYCHOLOGY, *6*(3), 237–246

The Reign of Peace

Mary Soledad L. Perpiñan
Third World Movement Against the Exploitation of Women
International Peace Research Association
Asia-Pacific Peace Research Association

This commentary on "A New Chance of Human Peaceableness?" affirms Elise Boulding as an eminent scholar, educator, advocate, practitioner, and believer in a God of peace. There are two parts to this commentary: (a) peace is in the heart, and (b) peace is at hand. The first part takes up the concepts of peace, harmony, and conflict from a feminist viewpoint. It cites how inner peace is achieved in the healing process of survivors of exploitation. It gives credit to Elise Boulding as a peace educator who draws from traditional practices and woman's culture. The second part focuses on the signs of hope that substantiate Kenneth Boulding's statement, "What exists is possible." These are current happenings such as (a) taking a stand as citizens, (b) mobilizing grass-roots, advocacy and service-oriented nongovernmental organizations, (c) forging global partnerships to meet supranational challenges, (d) having wider support for a stronger United Nations; and (e) imaging among faith communities.

To Elise Boulding's question, "A New Chance for Human Peaceableness?" I answer with hope for peace in the new millennium and affirm what Kenneth Boulding stated, "What exists is possible."

Elise Boulding is objective but being objective is not synonymous with being apolitical. She is far from being apolitical. She dares to be critical. For instance, she gives her assessment of the Hague Appeal for Peace (HAP) event in May 1999 as "a glaring failure to live up to the purposes of the conference". A good number of us HAP participants wanted the assembly to condemn the NATO bombing going on at that moment in Yugoslavia. We were aware of the "bureaucratic shortcuts and compromises with representatives of the major powers" and felt helpless. We also rued the fact that we failed to go next door to lobby at the International Court of Justice where matters regarding the Balkan situation were being decided concurrently with our assembly. Perhaps we would be just as powerless without

Requests for reprints should be sent to Mary Soledad L. Perpiñan, 1043 Aurora Boulevard, Quezon City, Philippines 1108. E-mail: perpinan@csi.com.ph

the creativity and courage of those behind the Seattle demonstration against the World Trade Organization.

The section on the United States' failure to say, "I'm sorry" for the atomic bombing of Hiroshima and Nagasaki is another case in point. I appreciate Elise Boulding's blunt statement that the United States "has never taken responsibility for having introduced *nuclear* warfare into the world and still unrepentantly holds a first-use-if-necessary doctrine." I am among those who strongly oppose the "bombing works" mentality of the American government. I grieved at the bombing of Iraq and the death-dealing embargo claiming the lives of thousands of children and innocent civilians. Thus I resonate with Elise Boulding who does not mince words when she says, "This sublimely self-assured military barbarism would appear to doom any possible spread of peace culture in the foreseeable future."

PEACE IS IN THE HEART

Elise Boulding speaks of peace culture as "a mosaic of identities, attitudes, values, beliefs, and institutional patterns that lead people to live nurturantly with one another and the earth itself without the aid of structured power differentials, to deal creatively with their differences, and share their resources."

A mosaic is made of pieces. Each piece in this case refers to a human person with a particular identity, a set of attitudes, values, and beliefs, integrated into some institutional pattern. Peace, therefore, begins in the core of a person's being. This interior peace is what is commonly called "peace of heart." When a person has a sense of well-being, confidence in one's self-worth, recognition of someone greater than the self, and respect for all those who share life in any form, then one can relate with humanity and the universe in peace with justice and love. It is a dynamic peace that I speak of, not the peace of the tomb. How can one be independent of the "structured power differentials" unless one has the courage to challenge unjust structures? Peace does not mean acquiescence to the status quo, especially if it is unjust.

I wrote about harmony and conflict in an article entitled "The Spirituality of Compassion: A Way to Peace." Here are some relevant lines:

> Letting conflict surface is not an act of peace breaking. Harmony does not always bring peace. If the majority is subservient to the minority of exploitative elite, there may be harmony. As long as the basic needs of the majority are not met, a state of peacelessness exists in the midst of external harmony. (Perpiñan, 1993, p. 2)
>
> Rocking the boat with protests against injustice can very well be an act of peace making. (Perpiñan, 1993, p.2)

In an earlier article, "Peace: A Breakaway from Patriarchy," I touched on the dominance system of patriarchy as the underlying cause of peacelessness in the individual, the community, the nation, the region, and the world. I identified the patriarchal roots of unrest as political and militarist expansion, cultural and religious oppression, and economic and ecological exploitation. I stressed that for peace based on justice, a feminist needs to identify with the downtrodden, the marginalized, the deprived, and even the depraved.

Elise Boulding mentions "bonding and autonomy." Let me draw from the experiences of the Third World Movement Against the Exploitation of Women (TW-MAE-W), which I head. In the TW-MAE-W ministry to survivors of the sex trade, incest, and rape, the experience of human bonding in a home where love is felt is the beginning of the healing process. Autonomy for our women and young girls would be the breaking of the shackles of exploitation and sexual abuse, freeing themselves from the sex industry, or from incestuous members of the household.

It is interesting to note how restorative justice, a term Elise Boulding used in the Truth and Reconciliation section of her article, can be applied to the healing process of the TW-MAE-W clientele. When a girl–child survivor of incest comes to us, seeking justice would mean filing a court case. When she wins the case, she has a sense of justice. But to be completely healed she has to learn to forgive. We are fortunate to have concrete cases of those who have gone through the full cycle of achieving justice, forgiveness, and reconciliation, where everyone—survivor, victimizer, members of the family, and our own TW-MAE-W community—enjoys peace of heart (Perpiñan, 1999)

Elise Boulding does not confine her work to scholarly research or erudite lectures in the academe and at international conferences. What edifies me is her practicality, her down to earth projects such as the current proposal to bring together "a team of peace educators, researchers and peace building practitioners from different world regions to explore the development of a curriculum guide." This would be a tool to help school children learn and live peace.

Learning from our own traditional practices, local processes, and resources is worth stressing. I have undertaken a conscientizing inquiry, sometimes referred to as participative research, among indigenous communities to surface their collective unconscious regarding peace and security. The richness of their heritage and their present crying needs lead to a reconceptualization of security and a vision of the kind of peace they would want to create in the future.

The importance given by Elise Boulding to woman's culture is much appreciated. I agree that such a culture is a carrier of peaceful behaviors that leads people to nurture one another and Mother Earth. Inner peace will thus radiate in ever widening circles.

PEACE IS AT HAND

Is there a basis for the millennial optimism exuded in the article of Elise Boulding? After the passing of the bloodiest century in human history, could we now look forward to the end of all wars and the reign of lasting peace? How can we overcome our cynicism and skepticism about the possibility of significant change? To Elise Boulding's credit, the comprehensive presentation of various efforts at peacebuilding is the fruit not only of scholarly research but also of the breadth and depth of the networking and advocacy work in which she has been engaged. She knows many of the people behind the movements and has had dealings with scores of nongovernmental organizations (NGOs). I share her pain at seeing NGO turfism and the many forms of self-promotion taking place in conferences. At this writing I am suffering from conference-fatigue and the futility of statements that do not really reflect the heart of the matter. Nonetheless, I would like to have a positive outlook and see the signs of hope that support her belief in a new chance of human peaceableness in the 21st century. Following are five positive signs, which can be considered actions.

Taking a Stand as Citizens

At the CIVICUS 3rd World Assembly held in Manila, Philippines from September 21st to 24th, 1999, some 700 participants from around 70 countries committed themselves as individual citizens—farmers, women, youth, trade unionists, indigenous peoples, and state and corporate reformers, among others. They resolved to expand their circles within their homes, neighborhoods, workplaces, communities, and nations. They called on governments, business firms, and civil society organizations to promote their popular demands to eradicate poverty by ensuring that every citizen's basic needs are met and to strengthen governance through an honest government that is fully accountable to its constituency. This was their global citizens' commitment to help build a civic world of equity and sustainability so that by the next millennium every home, village, town, city, and country will be safer, healthier, more egalitarian, and more sustainable. This is their stand for human security.

More than 1,000 NGOs gathered in Seoul, South Korea to build on the work begun at the United Nations (UN) World Conferences of the 1990s; forge a common vision for the 21st century; and channel their collective energy and experience to make this vision a reality.

They came up with "An Agenda for Peace, Security, and Development in the 21st Century." In the section on Peace and Security, the NGOs committed themselves to

1. Endorse the Hague Agenda for Peace and Justice for the 21st century.
2. Actively participate in the following specific international campaigns.
   - The ratification and implementation of the Ottawa Treaty to ban landmines.
   - The abolition of nuclear weapons.

- The Optional Protocol for the Convention on the Rights of the Child to raise the minimum age of military recruitment from 15 to 18 years.
- The ratification of the Rome Statute for the establishment of an independent International Criminal Court.
- The end to the trade and traffic in small arms.
- The international decade for a culture of peace and nonviolence for the children of the world, an Appeal by the Nobel Prize Laureates for the Children.

3. Promote active nonviolence and respect dignity of all people and try to ensure that no leader or dictator can commit crimes against humanity with impunity.
4. Create positive "Peace Zones" in all places now called "neutral" where people of all ages may receive medicine, food, and other humanitarian assistance and engage in activities that promote peace.
5. Call on member states of the UN to establish a standing UN police force.
6. Urge the UN to engage in speedy and effective intervention with humanitarian forces, subject to prescriptions of the UN Charter, when civilians are threatened by genocide, crimes against humanity, war crimes, and natural disasters.
7. Promote peace through education programs in schools and universities as well as engage in an intergenerational dialogue and awareness-raising toward the promotion of a culture peace.
8. Advocate for the creation of an effective mediation conflict prevention panel in the UN General Assembly with the task of promoting specific peace initiatives.
9. Urge that women, youth, and victims be seated at the peace negotiation table and be actively involved in planning and implementing efforts toward resettlement, rehabilitation, reconciliation, and in building sustainable peace.
10. Enable a civilian force trained in gender and cultural sensitivities, as well as local languages and other relevant skills, to accompany peacekeeping forces (NGLS Roundup, 1999).

This Jubillenium Commitment 2000 (jubillenium is a combination of "jubilee" and "millennium") is a pledge of individuals to respect all life, reject violence, share with others, listen to understand, preserve the planet, and rediscover solidarity.

Mobilizing Grass-Roots, Advocacy and Service Oriented NGOs

Writing about the massive emergence of NGO activities throughout the world, Tatsuro Kunugi (1999) noted the following chief comparative advantages of NGOs: (a) "they can provide quick and flexible response, and (b) not being mired in the sovereignty principle like the UN, they can 'fly under the radar' and involve themselves in internal situations including conflicts, massive violations of human rights, impending disasters whether natural or human-made."

Kunugi gives as example how innovative and pioneering "NGOs with grassroots knowledge of the psychological dimensions of local conflicts may be able to play the role of 'tug boat for the UN's ocean liner.'" Likewise, the cooperation of local NGOs, which have the know-how for environmental management of their domains or are in a position to call on traditional culture and wisdom for conflict resolution, may prove to be very useful in dealing with complex emergencies. In the academic community, research institutes can provide early warning based on empirical studies and future research on the evolving situation." (Kunugi, 1999, p. 10)

Forging Global Partnerships to Meet Supranational Challenges

"All together, we can. More than ever, the world needs the whole world ... The United Nations system is the world guarantee for the people's voice of all the countries to count in global governance" (Mayor, 1999). Federico Mayor, former head of the United Nations Educational, Scientific, and Cultural Organization, reaffirmed his belief in the UN in his speech at the World Civil Society Conference (WOCSOC) on "Building global governance partnerships" in December 1999.

Another speaker, Cornelio Sommaruga, president of the International Committee of the Red Cross, focused on global *humanitarian* action, which he defined as "any action taken to relieve any form of human suffering, whether caused by natural disasters or by man, in situations where individuals and communities are unable to cope on their own, and where international humanitarian agencies are compelled to act in order to save lives, alleviate suffering, restore basic human rights, and foster compliance with international law" (Sommaruga, 1999, p. 3). He hopes that in the 21st century this will be done swiftly, efficiently, impartially, without discrimination of any kind, and independent from political considerations so that emergency humanitarian action will not be used to pursue political ends.

"Global governance partnerships," stresses Wangari Maathai in her keynote address at WOCSOC, "will have to be democratic at all levels and with enforceable laws for all peoples and states. If it is democratic, it is not forced upon the weak by the powerful but is rather, for the common good of all." (Maathai, 1999)

The Women's Caucus at the WOCSOC came out with a statement of a women's vision of a new form of partnership:

> The word "partnership" has been tossed around by governments, the UN, donor agencies. And yet partnership can have streaks of patriarchy: subtle dominance,

> discrimination and undemocratic ways. The partnership that we envision should be characterized by mutuality, equality, and inclusivity.
>
> Our mission is to create that atmosphere at all levels—among our grassroots constituents, within national and regional networks, as well as with the international powers-that-be who claim to be our partners.
>
> Our goal is to make each one of us feel confidence in one's self-worth, in our capacity to break shackles that enslave us, and in our freedom to create alternative processes and structures.
>
> Only then can we have genuine governance that leads to a millennium of peace, justice and love. That is the spirit of Montreal that we would like to bring home. (Women's Caucus, 1999)

Having Wider Support for a Stronger UN

There is a growing sentiment in civil society expressed in international gatherings not only to support the UN, but above all to restructure it, so that it may have more political clout.

The 3rd Assembly of the UN of the Peoples in Perugia, Italy, from September 23rd to 25th, 1999, demanded that governments and parliaments give impulse to the development and to contextual democratization of the United Nations, beginning with the following measures:

- Reform the Security Council in a representative and democratic way.
- Promote the control on the legitimacy of the acts of the Security Council by the International Court of Law.
- Set up the Parliamentary Assembly of the UN as a subsidiary organism of the present General Assembly.
- Extend the fields of co-decision-making, which involve NGOs; institute at the UN headquarters a "permanent forum of global civil society" which could allow a stable coordination of the supranational organizations of citizens.
- Make the national delegations tripartite—executive, parliament, civil society—in the various organisms of the UN (Tavola della Pace, 1999).

Ramesh Thaku and Hans van Ginkel (1999) of the United Nations University, Tokyo, pin their hopes on the UN to actualize their aspirations for a future where men and women live at peace with themselves and in harmony with nature. Working with the people of the world, the UN, they believe, is "surely the best roadmap on offer to lead us out of hell on earth. Who knows as we step over the threshold into the new millennium, we may even stumble into heaven on earth: a better life in a safer world, for all." (Thaku & van Ginkel, 1999)

Imaging Among Faith Communities

What made the Seventh General Assembly of the World Conference on Religion and Peace (WCRP), held in Amman, Jordan, from November 25th to 29th, 1999, different, was the element of faith in a being greater than oneself. It was faith in a God who acts and saves. And the response was the collective endeavor to bring to reality the reign of this God through action for common living. This belief and commitment to action shone in all the plenary speeches of King Abdullah of Jordan, Prince Hassan, the elected chair of the conference, and the illustrious religious leaders of all faiths. The periods of quiet reflection and the varied rituals helped the participants interiorize the messages of peace.

Then came the sharing of best practices. The Sierra Leone interfaith endeavor to reconcile the rebel forces and reintegrate them to normal living was particularly striking. The interchurch efforts exerted to bring peace in the Balkan region was also impressive. Wanting to move forward in the direction of national peace, the Indonesian delegation led by President Wahid himself had its own special caucus to chart a new course with assistance from the religious communities.

I joined the WCRP Commission on Security and Disarmament. It was a small group but a good number of the members were former diplomats, notable of whom was Ambassador (Ret.) Jonathan Dean, International Security Adviser, Union of Concerned Scientists. Ambassador Dean presented the program of the Global Action to Prevent War and listed the following priorities for the years 2000 to 2005:

1. Establish a corps of 50 professional mediators at the disposal of the UN Secretary General and the Security Council.
2. Establish a Conflict Prevention Committee in the UN General Assembly.
3. Establish a standing volunteer police force at the UN, initially consisting of 2,000 men and women.
4. Promote the worldwide ratification of the treaty establishing the International Criminal Court, making government officials individually accountable for abusive human rights treatment of their citizens when local courts fail to act.
5. Ensure that the United States and other dues delinquents must pay their UN dues to finance the aforementioned activities.
6. Promote a worldwide freeze of armed forces.
7. Reduce nuclear arsenals to small immobilized stocks of nuclear warheads, separating warheads from delivery systems and storing both under international monitoring, to eliminate surprise attack or accidental use of nuclear weapons and to move decisively toward nuclear disarmament.

Ambassador Dean strongly believes that war is curable. Through a worldwide coalition to stop armed conflict and genocide, countries that have the resources and knowledge can drastically cut the level of armed violence in the world and make war increasingly rare. (Dean, 1999)

Each of the WCRP commissions has doable programs of action for the next 5 years. It was great to see the participants transcend differences and unite under the aegis of a God of peace, Yahweh, Allah, the same Being who dispenses the Hindu-Jainist-Buddhist "shanti," the Chinese "ho p'ing-p'ing ho," the Japanese "heiwa-wahei," the Korean "pyong-hwa," and the Filipino "kapayapaan," to permeate the total reality from the personal to the cosmic.

In the Judaic–Christian tradition, the year 2000 is a Jubilee year, a time for releasing the slaves, recalling the debt, restoring the land to the original owners, resting the earth—to which we add a fifth ethic, reclaiming the feminist principle (Perpiñan, 1997b).

By the Sea of Galilee, an impressive end-of-the-millennium event took place from November 21st to 23rd, 1999: the Jubillenium Interfaith Conference on World Peace. This was a spiritual and cultural gathering, highlighted by candlelighting at Kursi, a very inspiring ritual that quickened the heart to live in peace. Among the eminent religious leaders present was the Dalai Lama of Tibet.

The setting in the Holy Land brought to mind the Prince of Peace, Jesus Christ. Two thousand years ago, he proclaimed, "The Kingdom of God is at hand." In feminist language, we speak of the reign of God. If God reigns, there is peace.

Already But Not Yet

In conclusion to Elise Boulding's query, "A new chance of human peaceableness?" the answer is, peace is already at hand but it is not yet here in its fullness. There certainly are local and global efforts at bringing about peace in the human heart and peace in the cosmic world:

- Ordinary citizens have taken a stand to eradicate poverty, to work for a comprehensive human security, and to demand a kind of governance that responds to their basic needs.
- Grass-roots leadership has been mobilized by service-oriented NGOs engaged in transformative action.
- Global partnerships have been forged to meet supranational challenges for human survival and for the preservation of the planet earth.
- A clarion call to support and restructure the UN has been sounded.
- Faith communities have joined hands to concretely create peace in conflict-ridden places and to bring to reality their vision of God's reign of peace in the here and now.

This is the rainbow of peace that ushers in the Third Millennium. Like Noah, we are warned, however, that the fullness of peace is yet to come. It remains to be a task, a very arduous, challenging task, for the peoples of all continents. Where human efforts fail, we pin our hopes in a strong belief that peace is also a gift, a free gift from a bountiful God who cares more than we do that lasting peace will finally reign someday.

REFERENCES

Dean, J. (1999). *Global action to prevent war."*

Kunugi, T. (1999). *Building global governance partnerships among governments, inter-governmental organizations and NGOs* (ADMP Series No. 35). Sophia University, Institute of Comparative Culture, Tokyo, Japan.

Maathai, W. (1999). *Building global governance partnerships.*

Mayor, F. (1999). *Year 2000, the international year for the culture of peace.*

NGLS Roundup. (1999). *1999 Seoul International Conference of NGOs.*

Perpiñan, M. S. (1991). *Peace: A breakaway from patriarchy.*

Perpiñan, M. S. (1993). *The spirituality of compassion: A way to peace.*

Perpiñan, M. S. (1996). *Conscientizing inquiry among Cordillera women.*

Perpiñan, M. S. (1997a). *Empowering marginalized women.*

Perpiñan, M. S. (1997b). *Preparing for the great jubilee.*

Perpiñan, M. S. (1999). *The fruits of the labor.*Sommaruga, C. (1999). *Building a global humanitarian partnership.*

Tavola della Pace. (1999). *Third assembly of the UN of the peoples.*

Thaku, R., & van Ginkel, H. (1999). *Towards a world civil society.*

Women's Caucus, WOCSOC. (1999). A new vision of partnership.

PEACE AND CONFLICT: JOURNAL OF PEACE PSYCHOLOGY, *6*(3), 247–252

Obstacles to Peace

Adam Curle
East Dulwich, London, England

The culture of peace, which has made great strides in the last few decades, vies with the culture of violence. But this malign culture has also developed strongly, as is shown by a global explosion of economic inequality and military violence. This has been helped by enormous technological advances and more open marketing. These factors also have the potential for helping the development of a peace culture, but are currently dominated by the lust for power and profit facilitated by these developments. But the inner resources, both generating and generated by, the movement for peace could dissolve the forces of violence in time to avoid devastating catastrophes of war and environmental disharmony. Time, as we know, will tell.

I am sorry that my reading of the signs of the times may seem less optimistic than that of my dearly loved and respected old friend Elise Boulding. I agree completely with her assessment of the good things that are happening, the brave inspirations, the fresh structures for developing international contact and cooperation, the nongovernmental organizations, peace education, and the active and dedicated work on problems of injustice, the environment, and peace by young people. Most of this is new and wonderful and inspirational and no one has contributed a tenth as much to these good things as Elise—but how do I assess it by comparison with the nuclear arsenals, the reeking mass graves of Rwanda, the destruction of Vukovar, the abattoir created of Sri Lanka during the Janata Vimukhti Peramuna insurrection, or the rising tide of violence worldwide at all levels from the mass insanity of wars in the African Great Lakes area to Cambodia, to cruelty in the family. Of course, such assessments must be to some extent subjective, based on what we have experienced; there are images I cannot erase which may cloud my judgement. But there are terrible statistics that we cannot deny.

In recent books, *Another Way: Positive Response to Contemporary Violence* (Jon Carpenter, Charlbury, 1995) and more recently *To Tame the Hydra; Undermining*

Requests for reprints should be sent to Adam Curle, 35 Melford Road, East Dulwich, London SE22 0AG, England. E-mail: gme87@dial.pipex.com

the Culture of Violence (Jon Carpenter, Charlbury, 1999), I have tried to explain some sources of violence which I do not feel are generally understood, and to suggest how I believe we can contribute to abating them.

In this article I shall outline some of what I believe to be the dangers posed by the culture of violence to the establishment of a dominant culture of peace. I believe that such a culture can triumph. I would not otherwise have spent the last half century working for it, often in conditions that were harsh and difficult, or continued to do so well into my 80s. But I would be failing my friends and colleagues—and my grandchildren—if I did not emphasise the danger that we might fail; that the forces of political and economic, supported at times by military, violence, plus the closely connected environmental disaster, might bring our hopes to nothing.

I intend, therefore, to outline what I believe to be the obstacles, in global society and our microcosmic selves, to the establishment of the culture of peace, and to go on to suggest possible counteraction.

I begin by considering the state of the world as a conflictologist, or whatever is the technical term for someone concerned with the study of violence. I have, in the last 40 years—exclusive of 5 spent as a soldier in World War II— been involved actively in a dozen wars in Asia, Africa, and Europe (the last being 6 years in the Balkans) usually as a would-be peacemaker of some sort, and once (in South Africa) in a resistance movement. During the last 10 or 12 years I have seen the character of war changing in ways which are now well recognised. They are internal (what used to be called "civil") wars; they are exceptionally brutal (as I have seen in Sri Lanka, Bosnia, and Rwanda); they are largely waged by warlords rather than statesmen (I would include those such as Milosovic in the first category); 90% of the dead are civilian; they are wars of peoples against peoples rather than between regimes; the "rules" of war are consistently flouted; they are chaotic and apparently largely purposeless, especially those in parts of Africa—Sierra Leone is a sadly suitable example; and abducted children are often employed as soldiers as in Mozambique and in the "Lords Resistance Army" operating in Southern Sudan. But the pattern is unfortunately well-known.

The rest of the world finds it extremely difficult to cope constructively with these conflicts. In the case of former Yugoslavia efforts by the United Nations (UN), the European Union, the Organisation for Security Cooperation in Europe (OSCE), and individual nations have proved singularly confused, dilatory, and ineffective, only to end in excessive use of violence leading to fallible (Bosnia) and dubious (Kosovo) settlements. Instead, a more determined course of competent nonviolent, even dangerous, action—such as greatly increasing rather than withdrawing the OSCE observers in Kosovo, could, if tried, have been the basis of a more stable peace.

But could it?

We have to examine the character of our unpeaceful world. Why, when we have developed in this century a most impressive array of international agencies aiming to secure the peace and well-being of humanity, have things gone so terribly wrong? If we look at any single outbreak of large-scale (or indeed individual) violence we can usually find some of the apparent causative factors; in Rwanda and Burundi, for example, the Belgian colonial rule favouring the Tutsis over the Hutus was clearly such a factor. But is there some common factor?

I am sure that in many disturbed situations there is such a factor. I refer to this as the Hydra, the morass of global economic and political interdependency where governments and businesses alike share a common purpose: the conflict-prone pursuit of power and profit. The individual war is like a painful boil that the UN or some other force eventually lances; but it breaks out again because treatment fails to clean the infection of the wider, perhaps global, bloodstream.

This infection is the globalisation of a new religion that has developed with the collapse of the old faiths of Communism and Empire coupled with the weakened influence of the Christian churches. This has spread widely and rapidly through the concurrent developments of electronic communication and technical mastery in almost every field of human expertise. The new religion (widely promulgated by Margaret Thatcher and Ronald Reagan, but to a greater or lesser degree now accepted by most of the "Western" nations) promotes value of the Hydra, if necessary backed by military force. I need hardly expand on this theme—comparable views were widely, if crudely, promulgated at the recent World Trade Organisation meeting in Seattle.

I will only give one example from my own experience. At one stage I was working on the development problems of Pakistan. The head of the U.S. aid mission was a friend of mine whom one day I found in a towering rage because the Senate had turned down his most important project. This would have been of inestimable value by improving the wheat crop in the Punjab. Why had it been rejected? Because the U.S. surplus of wheat would then lose one of its best markets. This was over 40 years ago; a sign of the unfeeling greedy dominance that was increasingly to typify the behaviour of the rich toward the poor. Even the World Bank and the International Monetary Fund, however benign their purpose, by applying their principles and practices, have destroyed countless cultures and hence social economies in the name of growth and development. And in doing so they have scattered widely the seeds of war.

But the state of the world does not entirely depend on its economic and political structures. The nature of its human inhabitants, with whom the structures are interdependent, also play their part. And they are highly important. We tend to believe, however, that specific individuals, the great religious or political leaders, are disproportionately responsible for the large-scale events that affect humankind. But in one way or another we are all involved. If we are to understand and attempt to affect these happenings, we must understand who and what we are.

All living creatures are wonderful, particularly we human beings with our evolved endowment of brain and nervous system. Through these, we have amazing abilities to control and regulate the body and its functions, but have little awareness of some levels of our potentials. Some of these may only become apparent in exceptional circumstances: emergencies that evoke unexpected courage or ingenuity, wisdom or happiness, creativity or compassion. These capacities may be further developed through purposeful effort, psychotherapy, meditation, or religious practice. However, perhaps most of us are little aware of them. If anything we have perhaps a vague feeling that "God" was somehow guiding or working through these potentials, but do not consider them as constituting integral functions of our nature.

It may be objected that there is no proof that we all possess these potentials. I can only say that I have never met anyone in whom they were completely absent. They might well, however, be so deeply buried under layers of ignorance, confusion, and pain as to be almost irretrievable. This ignorance almost universally affects human attitudes and behaviour, although of course with considerable cultural variations .Most of us suffer an obscure sense of loss, guilt, or both; a feeling that something is missing and that we are to blame for its absence. (This may be heightened in some societies where belief in original sin is strong, or in some individuals whose childhood treatment has left them feeling unlovable, and therefore bad, because unloved.)

In addition—again with some cultural variability—we each think of ourselves as being separate, self-existent, and essentially lonely, individuals. Individuals we indeed are, but composite beings built up from our parents' genes, the nature of our society, our learning environment, and the human influences playing on us. Thus, although Jane Jones and Sid Smith are recognisable as distinctive, they are an amalgam of countless elements, genetic, social, educational, and experiential, and linked to the countless other individuals and influences that have formed them.

In fact we take our places in the world endowed with great natural gifts, but also with disadvantages derived from our failure to recognise and make full use of them. Together with the resultant sense of loss and guilt, we experience a measure of unhappiness, ranging from slight to depressive.

To the extent that we experience these differing degrees of unease or fault, we seek compensation. One form is based on the illusion of separate existence. It is important for our sense of self and security that this entity, this "I", should be identifiable as *Someone.* Depending on our tastes and interests this person should be a *special* person because of some quality or ability that is distinctive. It need not be something obviously desirable (the boast of one unfortunate friend of mine was that he had been in a maximum security gaol, not some ordinary clink); this singled him out in his own mind as someone special, as someone with an identity. Such are the criteria of reality or goodness to counteract the nonreality or badness of guilt and half-felt ignorance.

Connected with this construction of what might be called the false identity is the quality of acquisition. The great athlete needs the inner sense of goodness, reality, and identity conferred by gold medals; the scholar needs good reviews and honorary degrees; and the great beauty needs the plaudits of fashion journals and admirers. In general, most people crave, however humbly, for power, possessions, and position according to the criteria of their own lives, culture, and position in society.

But all means chosen to counteract existential angst are fallible and impermanent. The athlete loses skill and agility, the beauty becomes old and wrinkled, the scholar is discredited, the powerful leader is deposed, and the infamous gangster is forgotten.

In fact the remedies have failed. What next? This is a serious identity crisis. What other ruse can we devise to survive what is tantamount to a loss of self? Virtually any other ruse will fail for a comparable reason. If we do not succumb to despair, we become angry. It was the fault of rotten circumstances, of unreliable or hostile individuals. We are filled with hate. These may, of course, be extreme words. Despair may in most cases merely be regret, hatred be dislike, anger be irritation. All negative feelings, however, even if weak, agitate the mind, clouding its perception to the essence of our being, to the reality of our great potentials.

To the extent that these potentials are inadequately fulfilled, our actions may become antisocial. Acquisitive greed, bad temper, self-absorption, dislike, resentment, and comparable feelings damage relationships in any setting. It could perhaps be argued that where the need to compensate for the sense of loss or of guilt impels people to hard work and business enterprise, some good might emerge. But this underlying motive makes for uneasy relations and questionable management.

Such issues of individual psychology have also, naturally, affected social and economic structures. No doubt, they have always done so. However, with the emergence of the modern state in Europe, and more recently of globalisation, psychological needs for acquisition and for power—both to acquire and to protect profit—have become increasingly crystallised in the form of financial and military organisations; and these have become inseparably interwoven with political structures. (I should perhaps mention that the great contemporary transnational corporations have become strong enough to be virtually independent of the control of any government.)

The economic forces, and in many nations the military, have become so dominant that they have invaded almost every aspect of ordinary life. Even the least mercenary of us are caught up in them. We come to accept, even though we may dislike, things unthinkable a few decades ago, such as shopping on the Internet. We are dimly aware, but ignore out of shame for our impotence, the fearful damage done to the environment by excesses in our quest for profit. I say "our" with intent, for many of us have shares in the guilty companies, or at least enjoy their products. And fewer still are conscious that this is, in a sense, what we are asking for. We quail at the thought of nuclear war, but forget that it is we who demand what we believe to be protection for what we have so eagerly acquired. We and our forebears have built the modern world. We relish its good things (though we know they have so often been purchased at the pain and poverty of others). To be fair, we increasingly regret the path we have taken, but we are responsible for losing the way; it would be too easy if we could just blame the governments, or our teachers, or our parents.

Beginning to understand these things brings us to the key question: what might we do to change them? The short immediate answer is to talk about and deepen our grasp of the issues. I believe that the best way to proceed is to set up small discussion groups (perhaps consisting of 8 to 10 people). The prime purpose of these would be to gain some insight into our own nature and capacities. It was thus that the change of mood, leading to the corresponding change of constitution, came in South Africa; ironically the leaders of this moral revolution were the clergy of the Dutch Reformed Church whose interpretation of the Bible was largely responsible for the profoundly anti-Christian Apartheid regime.

Such changes of understanding undoubtedly demand meditation as well as intelligent discussion. I do not, by meditation, mean some necessarily "religious" practice, but some mental exercise that stills the constant flicker of thoughts across the screen of consciousness, giving greater scope for the play of our capacities; this can be achieved through some system of, say, yoga or prayer, or an emergency that releases a spontaneous reaction of courage or sympathy. There are of course a number of methods of meditation and it is up to individuals to choose one with which they are comfortable (emergencies cannot, obviously, be planned!). I believe, however, that it is important to think of the meditation as purposeful, as a service to suffering humanity through the growth of understanding, not just as calming and clearing the mind of the individual mediators. These, of course, would be women and men who were drawn to the wider cause of global harmony, not just as protesters but as individuals with some grasp of the extraordinary complexity of the issues at stake.

It is important to recognise that meditation is not *thinking about things*, but allowing the mind to rest on whatever are the particular topics involved. Take, for example, the conflicts of economic interests in which the good of one group is purchased at the expense of another. There may appear to be no way of resolving the issues satisfactorily for both parties, but the wisdom of the calm mind, no longer straining for a purely intellectual solution, may suggest some more telling lateral answer.

The myriad problems that face the world and its countless economic, political, and other human conundrums demand responses calling on our highest potentials not only for wisdom, but also for sympathy, because it is otherwise impossible to respond adequately to the needs of the world; courage, because our "revolutionary" (though nonviolent) approach may offend powerful interests; happiness, because without it, our message will be cool and uninspiring and we ourselves austere and humourless.

It is impossible to go beyond this point; the future will evolve in ways that cannot be predicted.

PEACE AND CONFLICT: JOURNAL OF PEACE PSYCHOLOGY, *6*(3), 253–258

Professor Boulding's Peaceable Kingdom

Peter Suedfeld
Department of Psychology
The University of British Columbia

An examination of Boulding's paper reveals questionable interpretations of historical as well as current events, and dubious extrapolations from these to the future. It is difficult to draw correct conclusions from false premises; the derogation of Western democracies and economic globalization, and the exaltation of movements that call themselves progressive and peace-enhancing—but are not necessarily either—place both negative and positive assumptions and presumed factors largely in the wrong places.

Elise Boulding's (2000) article is reminiscent of the famous painting, "The Peaceable Kingdom," by Edward Hicks, the 19th century Quaker preacher and artist. Although he produced around 100 versions of the picture, with numerous variations, the basic scene is always an American landscape inhabited by two or three children and a group of animals including both herbivores (lambs, cattle) and predators, with a large lion as the center of attention (Ford, 1998). Especially in its early versions, the scene is so eerie that although the lion lay down with the lamb, many viewers consider it unlikely that the lamb will be getting up again—and we worry about those children.

The word–picture presented by Boulding, although more nuanced than the painting, tries to convince us that the world is moving toward that idyllic scene. It takes a great deal of optimism to make this suggestion a year before the end of the most violent century in history, at least as measured by the number of victims killed deliberately in the course of war and persecution and probably even by the number of separate conflicts. It also takes some remarkable interpretations of historical and current events. No data are presented and evaluated to test Boulding's

Requests for reprints should be sent to Peter Suedfeld, Department of Psychology, The University of British Columbia, 2136 West Mall, Vancouver, BC V6T 1Z4 Canada. E-mail: psuedfeld@cortex.psych.ubc.ca

optimistic view. She has merely selected developments and events that suit her hypothesis, extrapolating from them to the future. Whether these are indeed the crucial trends that will shape that future, there is no way to tell; the article is an expression of personal opinion. My own comments consist of counter-examples and counter-arguments, which I consider to shake Boulding's propositions. However, history and current events offer a wide variety of items to choose from, and the choices are difficult to validate empirically. Boulding and I are far apart on sociopolitical as well as factual grounds, and my commentary is affected by my own perspectives; but the points of disagreement may at least alert the reader to the location of arguable assertions. In my opinion, the article places hope where it should not, and registers disapproval about major developments that may in fact make things better. In response to the journal's request for a "visionary article," Boulding has produced a utopian one. However, one must be careful to avoid the fundamental attribution error, or correspondence bias (e.g. Ross, 1977) or assuming that the source of an utterance is necessarily saying what he or she really believes. The article may respresent only Boudling's attempt to satisfy the need for being visionary. Therefore I would ask the reader to remember that when for the sake of brevity I refer to "Boulding," or to "Boulding's view/opinion/assertion," I really mean the opinions expressed in this particular article rather anything I know to be her actual opinion.

Boulding's definition of a peace culture incorporates important features whose relation to peace is questionable. If she really believes that a worldwide culture without "structured power differentials" is emerging, I can only wonder where it is. Throughout human history, there have been only a handful of communities, comprising only handfuls of people, where such hierarchies have not existed. Most of these were essentially artificial, utopian villages, usually based on religious dogma, and went out of existence fairly quickly in any historical time scale. There is certainly no sign of a cascade of such arrangements in the important components of the world system, whether governmental or private sector.

The examples that supposedly epitomize peace culture are puzzling, where they are not wrong. Don't peace churches, for example, have power differentials? Yes, they do; most have ministers and elders (by whatever name), and in all, some people are more influential than others. Are play and beauty incompatible with war? Hardly; war and violent conflict are the themes of many popular games among children; the arts, music, theater, and literature dealing with or springing from experiences of war are not inferior to those focusing on peaceful pursuits.

The exaltation of indigenous peoples on the basis of their closeness to nature, and of women's culture, is equally questionable. Whatever may be true of the Mbuti, indigenous people have since prehistoric times devastated their environment, eradicated a large number of animal and plant species, and busily killed, tortured, and enslaved each other (Axelrod & Suedfeld, 1995; Edgerton,1992; Preece, 1999). The Mongols, Tartars, Vikings, Zulus, Aztecs, Maoris, Tasmanians, Cheyenne, and so forth—dedicated warriors all—were "indigenous peoples." Peacefulness, like egalitarianism, has been limited to small marginal cultures, generally isolated from strangers; you can't have a war if you don't know anyone to fight. This is not, however, a realistic model for the world. I also don't believe that "introducing Nature as a teacher" will provide a great model of peace. As those who have actually lived in it (or have watched nature shows on television) are fully aware, Nature really is "red in fang and claw," and is completely indifferent to human values, aspirations, and ideals.

Women have been active fighters in many armed movements, and have perpetrated torture and genocide, from tribal wars in North America, Asia, and Africa, to the Nazi and Soviet concentration camps and the anticolonialist revolutions of the late 20th century. They have committed or attempted historic assassinations, including those of Jean-Paul Marat, Vladimir I. Lenin, and Gerald Ford. In every major war in this century, they have not only participated but urged their male relatives and fellow citizens to do so, too—white feathers were indeed publicly handed out by women to civilian male passers-by during World War I. Although their participation in organized violence continues, women (especially young women) are currently also escalating their involvement in violent crime. It may be argued that these examples do not really represent "women's culture," that *true* women's culture is peaceful. But then, the claim that women's culture contributes to peace becomes completely circular: if any traditional female behavior that involves violence is ruled out of "women's culture" by definition, then obviously it is true that women's culture is peaceful, but it is true only by definition. The same tactic could just as easily be applied to "men's culture."

Is the increasing salience of nongovernmental organizations (NGOs) really something to celebrate? Some NGOs, yes. The Red Cross, *Médecins sans Frontiéres*, Amnesty International, Oxfam—although they have their faults—have improved and lengthened the lives of injured, displaced, deprived, and persecuted individuals and groups around the world, and are likely to continue doing so. Popular and populist peace movements, springing up in places of actual conflict and repression, may do so, too: in Northern Ireland and the Philippines, for example.

By the same token, other NGOs are detriments to peace. The United Nations (UN) defines an NGO as "any non-profit, voluntary citizens' group which is organized on a local, national or international level" (UN Department of Public Information, 1999). That definition includes many terrorist, irredentist, and revanchist organizations that commit or support violence around the world. Even NGOs that claim to work for global pacification can be counterproductive. As one example, the European nuclear disarmament movement, had it succeeded, would have left the Western democracies at a definite disadvantage vis-à-vis an aggressive, oppressive, and fully armed Soviet Union. This, as we have since discovered, is why the KGB funneled funds to some of these groups (Andrew & Gordievsky, 1990;

Andrew & Mitrokhin, 1999). The proliferation of "ethnies," and the growth of ethnic, racial, gender, and so forth ("identity"), politics, are sources of danger, not hope. The rise in ethnopolitical warfare and terrorism, which has affected every continent except Antarctica, is the consequence of these ethnic NGOs crisscrossing national boundaries. Rwanda, Bosnia, Chechnya, Kashmir, Sri Lanka, and other hot spots offer ample evidence of this, as does the notable absence of interethnic reconciliation and solidarity as identity politics flourishes in just about every multiethnic country, including the United States.

Like many intellectuals, Boulding confuses words with reality. Government officials delivering public apologies do not always really regret the actions they are apologizing for (much less do they necessarily reflect the feelings of their citizenry). Organizations with the word "peace" in their name don't always support peace, and have sometimes been unwitting or even knowing fronts for bellicose governments or NGOs. Regardless of what treaties are signed, neither land mines nor nuclear weapons are likely to disappear as long as they are useful. In fact, the latter are becoming available to more and more governments and, even more scarily, to some NGOs. A UN declaration of years and decades for peace education will not abolish the military drill undergone by school children in the People's Republic of China, in North Korea, in Palestine, and many other places around the globe; and it will not stop the conscription of children and adolescents into both revolutionary and counterrevolutionary armed forces.

I don't want to belabor every one of Boulding's belaborable points; but there is another set, related to the history of World War II, that I cannot ignore. One component is her acceptance of the thesis that the nuclear attacks on Hiroshima and Nagasaki were superfluous. This is a complex and controversial issue. There may be "much evidence" supporting the assertion, but there is also much evidence to the contrary (e.g., Ferrell, 1996; Weintraub, 1995). The second is the comment about the "internment" of Japanese–Americans (only enemy aliens and people who explicitly rejected loyalty to the United States, about 13% of those relocated, were actually interned). The relocation is another complicated and arguable event (see Conn, 1989; Rehnquist, 1998); in retrospect, we may know it to have been unnecessary, but it certainly was not "arbitrary." I will pass over Boulding's most grotesque suggestion, that the Allies should apologize for the destruction required to defend themselves and the world in the war begun by the Axis powers.

I am not completely negative about Boulding's analysis. The work of Kelman, Staub, and other social–behavioral scientists, the recently established Ethnopolitical Warfare Initiative of the American and Canadian Psychological Associations, and academic and quasi-academic institutions in many countries focusing on conflict resolution, may ameliorate the ravages of armed conflict. Some NGOs are indeed making progress, and some people (possibly even some governments) may change their behavior in response to the UN and other peace-oriented organizations. Reconciliation programs may actually help heal the scars of conflict and prevent recurrences. The major difficulty is that it will take a long time for these trends to have significant impact on the occurrence of armed clashes: violence is still an obvious and in many ways inviting road to getting what one wants in material terms, and perhaps even more so as an expression of anger, despair, envy, frustration, fear, hatred, and prejudice.

What about the short run—say, the next 50 or 100 years? My own judgment is that the best hope for peace in the near future comes from two sources that Boulding disparages. One is the West, including what Boulding calls "the westernized mass media"; the other is the global economy. The former serves as an imperfect, but still the world's best, model of systems which promotes both individual freedom and political democracy, and its influence is spreading. In the past 50 years, dictatorships have completely disappeared from the map of Europe and almost completely from Latin America (except for Cuba). Asia and Africa are still infested with them, but even there democracy seems to be on the rise; and, as we know, democracies have rarely, if ever, gone to war with each other. In spite of the efforts of some United Nations Educational, Scientific, and Cultural Organization members to censor them, the media, including the Internet, spread visions based on such systems to the parts of the world that are oppressed and tyrannized, making it more and more difficult to keep the people from demanding a change.

At the same time, the media also proliferate images of a life with abundant material goods —that old devil, the "greedy consumer culture." This may seem undesirable to the comparatively rich people of the West (which includes most people in the West, and certainly all Western academics), but it is perfectly reasonable and just for the impoverished citizens of the "Two-Thirds World" to aspire to a materially better life. Again, not perfectly, but slowly and with many setbacks, the globalization of trade and production will make this possible. To the extent that poverty, or relative poverty, is a source of conflict, that source will become less potent; and, to put it crassly, people who are busy working toward a better life for themselves and their family may become less likely (and have less time) to take up arms and destroy the lives and property of others.

This has been happening, and will continue to happen, under the protective armed umbrella of the United Nations, NATO, and other organizations primarily influenced and financed by the Western democracies. As they did in two recent actions criticized by Boulding (in 1990 to 1991 in the Persian Gulf, perhaps deterring future military invasions of defenseless neighbors, and in 1999 in Yugoslavia, perhaps deterring future undertakings of ethnic cleansing, mass rape, and genocide), those democracies, still making some errors, but getting it right most of the time, will continue to sacrifice their own blood and treasure to foster peace by opposing those who start wars, even if the only effective way to oppose them is by going to war oneself.

REFERENCES

Andrew, C. M., & Gordievsky, O. (1990). *KGB: The inside story of its foreign operations from Lenin to Gorbachev*. London: Hodder & Stoughton.

Andrew, C. M., & Mitrokhin, V. (1999). *The sword and the shield: The Mitrokhin archive and the secret history of the KGB*. New York: Basic Books.

Axelrod, L., & Suedfeld, P. (1995). Technology, capitalism, and Christianity: Are they really the three horsemen of the eco-collapse? *Journal of Environmental Psychology, 15,* 183–195.

Conn, S. (1989). *United States Army in World War II: Western hemisphere, guarding the United States and its outposts*. Washington, DC: U.S. Government Printing Office.

Edgerton, R. B. (1992). *Sick societies: Challenging the myth of primitive harmony*. New York: Free Press.

Ferrell, R. H. (Ed.). (1996). *Harry S Truman and the bomb: A documentary history*. Worland, WY: High Plains.

Ford, A. (1998). *Edward Hicks, painter of The Peaceable Kingdom*. Philadelphia: University of Pennsylvania Press.

Preece, R. (1999). *Animals and nature: Cultural myths, cultural realities*. Vancouver, Canada: University of British Columbia Press.

Rehnquist, W. H. (1998). *All the laws but one: Civil liberties in wartime*. New York: Knopf.

Ross, L. (1977). The intuitive psycholoist and his shortcomings; Distortions in the attribution process. In L. Berkowitz (Ed.), *Advances in experimental social psychology* (Vol. 10; pp. 174–221). New York: Academic Press.

UN Department of Public Information (1999). Retrieved January, 2000 from the World Wide Web: http://www.un.org/MoreInfo/ngolink/brochure.htm

Weintraub, S. (1995). *The last great victory: The end of World War II, July/August 1945*. New York: Dutton.

PEACE AND CONFLICT: JOURNAL OF PEACE PSYCHOLOGY, *6*(3), 259–266

Toward a Global Movement for a Culture of Peace

David Adams
Director, Unit for the International Year for the Culture of Peace UNESCO

The culture of peace concept has been developing for 10 years at the United Nations Educational, Scientific, and Cultural Organization and the United Nations (UN) since it was first described at Yamoussoukro in 1989. It calls for a transformation and development of alternatives to the values, attitudes, and behaviours that are necessary and sufficient for the preparation and elaboration of the culture of war and violence: the concept of power as force; the image of an enemy that does not have the same rights as you; authoritarian social structure, secrecy, and armaments. The UN, in its recent Declaration and Programme of Action on a Culture of Peace, has called for a global movement for a culture of peace. This commentary describes unique aspects of this movement, as well as actions designed to launch and promote its development.

Having been involved with the culture of peace concept at the United Nations Educational, Scientific, and Cultural Organization (UNESCO) and the United Nations (UN) since the 1989 event at Yamoussoukro mentioned by Elise Boulding, I should like to begin by describing the road taken to develop this concept at the governmental and intergovernmental level. In doing so, I do not wish to underestimate the important role of the nongovernmental organizations (NGOs) and of individuals that, as she describes, are also essential. In fact, the culture of peace, like those of human rights and of sustainable development (both, in fact, components of the culture of peace) is a concept that enables these four levels of social organization to unite their energies in a common "global movement for a culture of peace" as we enter a new century and millennium.

Resolutions adopted on four dates stand out as signposts along this road:

Requests for reprints should be sent to David Adams, Director, Unit for the International Year for the Culture of Peace, UNESCO, 7, place de Fontenoy, Paris 75352, France. E-mail: d.adams@unesco.org

- October 1992, the 58 Member States of the UNESCO Executive Board welcomed the concept of a culture of peace and called for its further development and expression in concrete activities(140 EX/Decision 5.4.2).
- November 1995, the 186 Member States of the 28th General Conference of UNESCO stated that the major challenge at the close of the 20th century is "the transition from a culture of war and violence to a culture of peace" (Resolution on the Medium-Term Strategy for 1996–2001).
- November 1997, the United Nations General Assembly adopted a resolution for the culture of peace (A/52/13) and another declaring the year 2000 the International Year for the Culture of Peace (A/52/15).
- September 1999, the United Nations General Assembly adopted a Declaration and Programme of Action on a Culture of Peace (A/53/243).

These decisions were the result of personal efforts by the Director-General of UNESCO during that period, Dr. Federico Mayor, and by the leadership at the UN General Assembly exerted by the Ambassador of Bangladesh, Mr. Awarul Chowdhury. It is my great privilege to have worked on this initiative with them as well as with many others who have played important roles.

The development of the concept along this road has not always been smooth and unanimous as it might seem from the surface. In fact, the conflicts concerned can be illustrated by examining the difference between the final version of A/53/243 as adopted and the draft that was submitted to the General Assembly one year before (A/53/370). The final version was the result of 9 months of intensive informal discussions at the UN General Assembly in which the differences among the Member States gradually became evident.

The states of the European Union took the position that there is no culture of war and violence in the world, and they succeeded in imposing their way so that all references to this had to be taken out of the final document. Ironically, this was during the war in Kosovo where the actions of NATO were guided especially by these same states. Why is there such objection by the most powerful states to the idea that there is a culture of war in the world today? My personal belief is that the opposition to the concept of a culture of war reflects a refusal to admit that powerful states today—just as they have been from the beginning of recorded history—depend on the culture of war to retain their power. A few years ago, I published an article in the *Journal of Peace Research* entitled "The History of Internal Military Intervention in the United States" (Adams, 1995). For the past 120 years in that country, there have been an average of 18 internal military interventions employing 12,000 troops per year. One of the conclusions that one may draw from the article is that the function of maintaining a military force is as important for maintaining internal power as defending against foreign invasion and defending foreign economic and political interests. Furthermore, those who oppose the power of the state from within can be suppressed on the basis of branding them agents of an enemy from outside.

Although, as a result of the Europeans' insistence, the final declaration for a culture of peace was substantially changed from that which had been suggested in A/53/370, at the same time, the framework of the program of action continued to reflect the basic concept that had been worked out within the framework of an analysis of the culture of war and violence.

AREAS OF ACTION FOR A CULTURE OF PEACE

There are eight areas of action that form the framework of the Programme of Action. Each of these eight areas is necessary for the transition from a culture of war and violence to a culture of peace and nonviolence. Each addresses a cultural aspect that is at the same time the result of war and violence and a condition that makes war and violence possible. In fact, the development of a culture of peace in the future would make it impossible for wars to be started. The eight areas of action are listed here in detail—first the wording in the adopted document (A/53/243), and then the background statement, as it is worded in the submitted document (A/53/370):

1. *Culture of peace through education.* "The very concept of power needs to be transformed—from the logic of force and fear to the force of reason and love."
2. *Sustainable economic and social development.* "This represents a major change in the concept of economic growth which, in the past, could be considered as benefiting from military supremacy and structural violence and achieved at the expense of the vanquished and the weak."
3. *Respect for all human rights.* "The elaboration and international acceptance of universal human rights ... calls for a transformation of values, attitudes and behaviours from those which would benefit exclusively the clan, the tribe or the nation towards those which benefit the entire human family."
4. *Equality between women and men.* "Only [the] linkage of equality, development and peace can replace the historical inequality between men and women that has always characterized the culture of war and violence."
5. *Democratic participation.* "This is the only way to replace the authoritarian structures of power which were created by and which have, in the past, sustained the culture of war and violence."
6. *Understanding, tolerance and solidarity.* "There has never been a war without an "enemy", and to abolish war, we must transcend and supersede enemy images with understanding, tolerance and solidarity among all peoples and cultures."
7. *Participatory communication and the free flow of information and knowledge.* " ... needed to replace the secrecy and manipulation of information which characterize the culture of war."
8. *International peace and security.* " ... peace diplomacy, peacekeeping, disarmament and military conversion. ... "

Although the UN Charter called in 1945 for the abolition of war, it has taken until now to formulate and call for the abolition of those values, attitudes, and behaviours of societies that all together are necessary and sufficient for the *preparation* for war: the concept of power as force; the image of an enemy that does not have the same rights as you; and authoritarian social structure, secrecy and armaments.

The transformation from a culture of war and violence to a culture of peace and nonviolence is perhaps more radical and far-reaching than any previous change in human history. Every aspect of social relations—having been shaped for millennia by the dominant culture of war—is open to change, from the relations among nations and between nations and their citizens to those between women and men. Everyone, from the centres of power to the most remote village, may be engaged in the process. In her article, Elise Boulding reveals many important aspects and consequences of this transformation.

CALL FOR A GLOBAL MOVEMENT FOR A CULTURE OF PEACE

How can the transformation be accomplished? Paragraph 6 of the Programme of Action on a Culture of Peace recently adopted by the UN General Assembly calls for a "global movement for a culture of peace," based on partnerships among states, international organizations, and the various actors of the civil society.

Like the great social movements of the past, such a movement should be based largely on the nongovernmental actors of the civil society whose role is correctly stressed by Dr. Boulding. This is appropriate because most NGOs, unlike the state, are not dependent for their power on the culture of war. Instead of maintaining power through force of arms, most of them gain their adherents and results by the force of their argument and gather strength through the mobilization of the righteous indignation of their members.

The formulation of the culture of peace is deliberately broad, to include the goals of the full range of NGOs working for peace and justice. These include human rights, sustainable development, democratic participation, and equality of women, as well as disarmament and nonviolent means for social change. In other words, we may see that people everywhere are already working for a culture of peace; they just don't call it by that name. The purpose of the culture of peace movement is to link together and hence strengthen the many movements that already exist. To quote Ambassador Chowdhury, it is a "grand alliance of existing movements" (Chowdhury, 1998).

Because of its fundamental principles this must be different from most of the great social movements of the past in at least one very important aspect. It must not create enemy images and must be essentially nonpartisan and open to working with everyone. It must be global in scope, based itself on the universality of values—the inalienable right of every human being to a life of peace and nonviolence.

It must not oppose the state and its institutions, but transform them through democratic means. Even military institutions should not be seen as the enemy, but efforts should be made to transform their practices from force to peacekeeping by nonviolent means.

The dynamics of the global movement for a culture of peace should, therefore, be different from the peace movements and social justice movements of the past. Rather than coming to an end through short-term victory, it should gather strength from each success leading toward a total social transformation. This is different from the past, when movements dedicated to the overthrow of a government came to an end with the formation of a new government or, if they were oriented against a particular war, they stopped with the end of the war. As a result of this pattern of rise and fall, as I found in my study of the great American Peace Movements, each peace movement in the past was unable to benefit from the leadership of its predecessors but had to develop totally new leadership (Adams, 1985). Movements were successful in ending particular wars and particular oppressive regimes, but the culture of war itself remained unchallenged and unchanged.

As in all successful movements, the basic principles and goals need to be simple and universal. For this purpose, the Nobel Peace Laureates have written the Manifesto 2000 (called Commitment 2000 in the article of Elise Boulding) by which each individual in the world is invited to make a commitment to follow the principles of a culture of peace in everyday life. In taking up the Manifesto 2000 the NGO Education International (representing 23 million teachers) remarked that these principles—presented here in abbreviated form—correspond to the basic rules of the school classroom:

- Respect all life.
- Reject violence.
- Share with others.
- Listen to understand.
- Preserve the planet.
- Rediscover solidarity.

As a fundamental act for the emerging movement, people are being asked to sign the Manifesto 2000. The full text of the Manifesto, along with a signature form, may be found on the Internet at http://www.unesco.org/manifesto2000. The Manifesto 2000 is not an appeal to higher authorities, but is a commitment by each individual to take action. It provides a simple, positive vision for the global movement for a culture of peace that can inspire and motivate people to take action. Although such a positive vision for the future has not been sufficiently prominent in many peace and justice movements of the past, as I have documented in my studies of consciousness development of peace activists, it is essential for this new type of movement (Adams, 1987).

Some will argue that the transition to a culture of peace and nonviolence is not possible because they believe that human beings are intrinsically violent. In fact, this attitude can be a "self-fulfilling prophecy," because studies have shown that if young people believe this, they are less likely to take action for peace. However, there is no scientific basis to believe that war is in our genes or in our human nature. The leading scientists in the relevant fields of psychology, sociology, anthropology, genetics, and brain research have come to the conclusion, in the words of the Seville Statement of 1986, that "the same species that invented war is capable of inventing peace" (Adams, 1991). In this regard it is important to distinguish violence from righteous indignation. In fact, there is a very strong tendency in most people to become angry and take action in the face of injustice. The great peace activists such as Gandhi, King, and Mandela have shown that such anger and action are essential for social movements, but the anger is more effectively expressed through nonviolent methods than violence. Training people how to distinguish violence from anger and how to take nonviolent action against injustice is a very important basic task of the movement for a culture of peace and nonviolence.

Launching of the Movement

To conclude, I will outline here the actions that UNESCO is undertaking to launch this global movement for a culture of peace. There are five stages in the process: (a) national endorsements; (b) media campaign; (c) partnerships for the Manifesto 2000 campaign; (d) development of a global network of local projects; and (e) global communication systems for the movement.

National endorsements have been received now from over 50 heads of state, either for the culture of peace in general or for the Manifesto 2000 in particular, and over 100 national delegations to the recent General Conference of UNESCO pledged their support to the culture of peace and the International Year for the Culture of Peace. Declarations that endorse the culture of peace have been made by international organizations and meetings throughout the world, including the Organization of African Unity and Association of South East Asian Nations.

A global media campaign was launched in conjunction with the opening day of the International Year for the Culture of Peace on September 14th, 1999, the International Day of Peace. A television spot featuring Nobel Peace Laureates and the principles of the Manifesto 2000 was distributed throughout the world and seen by millions of people. Events were held in over 100 countries, most of them carried by national media. A synopsis of these events is now available on the Internet (www.unesco.org/iycp). The television and radio spots will be continued throughout the year 2000 to sensitize public opinion that the movement is underway and they are available to any organization that agrees to be a partner for the Year. In the United States these requests for partnership should be addressed to the Office of UNESCO at the UN in New York.

A global campaign is underway to gather signatures on the Manifesto 2000 with a goal of presenting 100 million signatures to the summit conference of heads of state that will take place at the Millennium Assembly of the UN in the fall of 2000. This is being done by developing a wide range of partnerships at both international and national levels. At the international level, a partnership agreement has been sent to the 341 NGOs associated with UNESCO (organizations such as Education International previously mentioned, the World Organization of Scout Movements, etc.). At the national level, a manual has been sent to all 180 UNESCO National Commissions, 60 field offices, and 150 UN national coordinators asking them to serve as focal points and to engage national organizations in the campaign. Mailings have been sent as well to 6,000 universities and over 1,000 cities. Just to give some idea of the scope of the campaign, 6 million leaflets have been distributed in Algeria and 800,000 in Barcelona and the Paris suburb of Saint Denis alone. Pledges of 5 million signatures have been received from the UNESCO Club movement of Africa, 1 million from the UN Association of the UK, the national focal point in that country, and 1 million from Japan. Organizations are invited to link their Internet Web sites with that of Manifesto 2000 (www.unesco.org/Manifesto2000) so that people can sign directly on the Internet. Already by the beginning of the year 2000, Algeria and Brazil had registered over one million signatures each.

On a national level, partnership agreements are being established with NGOs, schools, universities, cities, parliaments, media organizations, and enterprises. In addition to the signature campaign for the Manifesto, each partner is asked to dedicate at least one major event to the International Year—hence developing a global calendar of events. They are also requested to provide information on local projects that promote one or another aspect of the culture of peace, which will be posted on the Internet.

A social movement, above all, is a process of collective consciousness development. It gains strength and achieves its goals to the extent that this consciousness development is shared and reinforced by communication at a mass level. Unfortunately, because of its close ties to the culture of war and violence, the mass media cannot be relied on to provide this communication, but the movement must develop its own independent and alternative communication systems. This is a lesson we have learned in mass movements of the past; for example, the civil rights and antiwar movements of the 1960s, and the revolutions in the Philippines, South Africa, and Eastern Europe in more recent years.

We are developing two such communication systems for the movement, both relying heavily on the Internet. The first was mentioned earlier (www.unesco.org/iycp). The accumulation and exchange of information on local projects for a culture of peace should develop throughout the next decade. In our system, each local project will be asked to provide information on what it is doing, what it needs, and what it can provide to others. This methodology has been worked out over the past few years for environmental groups belonging to the Internet network called Planet Society.

The second system is more ambitious: to develop a global network of Internet sites in various languages that will provide up-to-date information from around the world on news events and media productions that promote the various aspects of a culture of peace and nonviolence. This is called the Culture of Peace News Network. It relies on the visitor to write reports and provides for the training of large numbers of volunteer "Culture of Peace Moderators" who work with the visitor to make their reports correspond to the "rules of the game," at which point they are put online. Each partner Web site agrees to send one moderated report a week to a central pool and to take one from that pool to put on their own Web site, translating them in and out of the language of their site. This will enable a global, multilingual system that is constantly updated.

The momentum developed during the International Year for the Culture of Peace (2000) will be continued into the Decade for a Culture of Peace and Nonviolence for the Children of the World (2001 to 2010); in fact partners for the Year are invited to participate in the preparation of the program of action for the Decade.

REFERENCES

Adams, D. (1985). *The American peace movements.* New Haven, CT: Advocate Press.

Adams, D. (1987). *Psychology for peace activists.* New Haven, CT: Advocate Press (Rev. ed., 1995, unpublished but available from David Adams).

Adams, D. (Ed.). (1991). *The Seville Statement on Violence: Preparing the ground for the constructing of peace.* Paris: UNESCO.

Adams, D. (1995). Internal military intervention in the United States. *Journal of Peace Research, 32*(2), 197–211.

Chowdhury, A. K. (1998, January). Culture of peace: A universal concept at the world body. *Keynote address at UNESCO, Paris* (available from Permanent Mission of Bangladesh to the United Nations).

PEACE AND CONFLICT: JOURNAL OF PEACE PSYCHOLOGY, *6*(3), 267–271

Response

Elise Boulding
Professor Emeritus of Sociology,
Dartmouth College

I am grateful for a stimulating and thought-provoking set of reflections in response to my essay on peaceableness. To be honest, I had a hard time writing that article. I had just finished the *Culture of Peace* book when Milton Schwebel's request came to me, and I felt "written out," empty. Yet I couldn't say no! I used a well-worn formula to jump-start my writing, by referring to the 1899 Hague Peace Conference as a promising start for the 20th century. In retrospect, I heartily agree with Cheryl de la Rey's caustic question, "promising start for whom?" I have often decried the premature universalism of the European internationalist movements of the 19th and early 20th century, which developed in complete ignorance of the history and values of the Two-Thirds World that Europe was colonizing. Indeed, there was much suffering in the early decades of the century just past, and structural asymmetries were indeed deepening. Shallow millennialism is dangerous. There will be no sudden outbreak of peace because of a particular date in one of the world's calendric systems.

The present call to build a Culture of Peace in 2000 is not, however, shallow millennialism, but a civic opportunity to call for a much more rigorous peace praxis based on a full recognition of the extent of social and economic injustice in today's world, coupled with a strong critique of the nature and uses of power. Because the problems are complex, it is a call to action for the long haul. Most of the comments address these basic issues, I am glad to say. I strongly agree with de la Rey's emphasis on the need for a better understanding of citizenship in civil society, which speaks directly to the matter of praxis. How do we empower the disempowered, and learn deeper lessons about social respect? De la Rey is right that I skimped on gender analysis. Sorry! But fortunately, both she and Sister Sol (Mary Soledad Perpiñan) have remedied that. It is true that calling attention to how the victimage of women is built into our patriarchal social structures needs to be

Requests for reprints should be sent to Elise Boulding, 44 East Plain Street, Wayland, MA 01778.

persistently and repeatedly brought out. However, it is also true that the development of the skills of civic participation and the claiming of public space by women is an indispensable part of the ending of that victimage. Far more activity by women in public spaces will be required if societies are to shift from the Rambo mode to creative problem solving in situations of violence and injustice. (And yes, Peter Suedfeld, it is important to recognize that there are female Rambos, just as there are men who are gentle saints. That is how we know that these two potentials coexist in every human being, and need to be carefully addressed.)

Caroline Lamwaka writes from the very front lines of battle in Uganda. She has seen peacebuilding projects dismantled time and again by soldiers and by guerillas, in a region where there is continuing glorification of war. And violence appears to win, in the short term. How does one build a political peace culture, she asks. Nongovernmental organizations (NGOs) often evade the difficult challenges and may actually hide behind humanitarianism. But Lamwaka recognizes that lack of education is a major disempowering factor, with an accompanying lack of skills of analysis and practice in civic and political problem solving. Peacebuilding is about developing undeveloped human potentials in local people in their home communities through every strategy that educators and practitioners can devise. It involves building and rebuilding after destruction until there is critical mass of educated men, women, and children to support a sustainable local and regional peace. Lamwaka's own education and training work in the project GULU HOPE in northern Uganda is a fine example that needs to be widely replicated and firmly supported.

Adam Curle (now in his 80s, as he points out) has spent a lifetime working for peace—often in very violent and difficult settings. He knows more about the obstacles to peace than many of us can even conceive. His image of the hydra, a morass of global economic and political interdependencies in pursuit of power and profit, goes to the heart of contemporary war-proneness. But Curle has never lost sight of a profound intuition about human potentials for living gently and peacefully on the planet. He continues to act on that intuition even now in the Balkans. How? By encouraging local groups to search together deeply and meditatively, to discover those hidden potentials. Adam Curle works with them in ways that create a new civic reality, islands of peace culture with room for human joy; islands that can connect and grow with a steadiness and persistence that violence, greed, and a will to power cannot match. He walks his talk.

Ursula Oswald Spring has long battled the hydra of malign globalization as a scholar–activist who has also served in government. Familiar with many different kinds of networks, she looks to alternative communication media to develop a very different kind of global interdependence. Like Curle, she would draw on human wisdom in new–old ways. Her emphasis on the intellectual, scientific, and moral capacities that have developed over the millennia in the world's civilizations, and on the rich cultural and ethnic diversity of our own era—what I would call the diversity of the 10,000 societies of the sociosphere—in a sense involves taking the same kind of careful look at the human potential that Adam recommends, and that I strongly support. Of course, the process of sifting over the accumulated cultures of past civilizations and today's ethnies has to be done with great care. Malign values and practices are scattered through those cultures, along with inspiring ones. Cultures of violence have arisen. That is precisely why a careful deep searching of collective human experience is necessary to choose the most appropriate building blocks for a culture of peace. Spring offers a politically activist version of Adam Curle's more meditative exploration. NGOs have an important part to play, but must move from the show-and-tell orientation that characterized the 1999 Hague Conference to a more hands-on actual collaboration in relation to specific social tasks.

I had a good laugh over Peter Suedfeld's opening comments on Quaker Edward Hicks's Peaceable Kingdom paintings, for indeed one of those paintings will adorn the jacket of my forthcoming *Cultures of Peace* book. Yes, he and I are far apart in world views, and each of us reads what the other writes with a certain sense of incredulity! Just as he would question my sources, I would question his (having read at least some of them). But on one thing we agree: conflict is a basic element of the human experience. (On the strength of that, do drop in for a cup of tea when you are in the Boston area, Peter.) The culture of peace concept does not include abolishing conflict, only changing the means for dealing with it.

Suedfeld feels that a "benign" use of military force, such as recently in the Persian Gulf and Yugoslavia, will be necessary to settle conflicts for the foreseeable human future. From my perspective, current military buildups in the United States and elsewhere and the accompanying rise in international tensions make less and less room (and leave fewer and fewer resources) for creative dispute resolution. But I do think that the ingredients are, nevertheless, there for the transformation of military forces into nonviolent peacekeeping forces, building on the best of the disaster-meeting capabilities that are already in the military. They, too, could become part of the culture of peace, shifting the current state security focus to a human security focus, with environmental protection as a key strategy. Jon Barnett, of the Center for Pacific Studies at the University of Canterbury, New Zealand, has spelled out this new type of security function for armies in a very illuminating way (Barnett, in press).

To get back to conflict itself, it is humanity's teacher. Lewis Coser, in *The Function of Social Conflict* (1956), pointed out that it is through the clash of conflicting interests and needs that insights become available that make problem solving possible. If so, then space needs to be created for the emergence of such insights, and the ripening of human wisdom, and the development of social skills, as both Curle and Spring point out in their commentaries. And I am happy to note that Suedfeld sees the value in the highly relevant interactive problem-solving work of Kelman and associates. Yes, such developments take time. Who can spell it out in centuries? There is an old Chinese saying that a journey of a thousand miles begins with a single step.

Sister Mary Soledad Perpiñan has worked at peace building in the Philippines and the world through many turbulent decades. Her words, "Rocking the boat with protests against injustice can very well be an act of peacemaking," give a welcome emphasis to the adventurous, risky, challenging aspects of peace work. Not the least adventurous of these activities has been her work with survivors of the sex trade, incest, and rape. These survivors can and do become coworkers in the building of peace culture on every continent. I particularly appreciate the ease with which Sister Perpiñan moves from local to the regional to the global. She knows well the pathways, secular, religious, nongovernmental, and intergovernmental. As she reminds us, communities of faith, both because of and in spite of their own histories of violence, have a special calling to activate the often-ignored peace and justice teachings that are present in every world religion. There is also a spiritual dimension to the human journey independent of all formal religious institutions, and the vitality of peace work continually draws on that dimension, whether explicitly or not. No culture of peace could survive without it.

I am grateful that David Adams found the time to provide an overview of the development of the Culture of Peace program at the UNESCO (United Nations Educational, Scientific, and Cultural Organization) and the United Nations (UN), both from the perspective of member states and of NGOs. The movement from rhetoric about ending war to a specific naming of eight concrete areas of action for creating the conditions of peace is potentially very empowering for NGOs. These action arenas include the goals of numerous peace and justice NGOs, and the program itself explicitly encourages partnerships and alliances among them and with states, as well. It is true that peace movements have historically tended to peak–trough cycles, and lost wisdom as well as momentum during trough years. If the "grand alliance" of NGOs can retrieve and build on their collective wisdom, this will indeed be a step forward in the strengthening of peace culture in the world. Regarding Manifesto 2000, addressed both to individuals and organizations, the dimension of commitment to action needs to be emphasized. Those who sign it are not just making another declaration, they are personally committing themselves and their organizations to work for a culture of peace. At best, the Manifesto will begin the process of collective consciousness development that will strengthen the intellectual, spiritual, and social action capacities of civil society to deal creatively and nonviolently with conflict at every level, from family and community to the UN itself. For that to happen, however, more than millennialist peace fervor is needed. It will take sustained effort to deepen thought and upgrade problem-solving skills of individuals of every age in every social sector—civic, professional, and governmental; not just for a decade, but for lifetimes and generations to come.

Yes, this is a best-case scenario for the human race. There are many worst-case scenarios available. I choose hope, grounded in a full recognition of all the obstacles to peace, and in the will to develop the wisdom and skills to overcome them. Why not choose hope?

REFERENCES

Barnett, J. (in press). "The meaning of environmental security: Environmental politics and policy," *New security era*. London: Zed Books.

Coser, L. (1956). *The function of social conflict*. Glencoe, IL: Free Press.

Anything that obscures the fundamentally moral nature of the social problem is harmful, no matter whether it proceeds from the side of physical or psychological theory.

John Dewey, 1939

PEACE AND CONFLICT: JOURNAL OF PEACE PSYCHOLOGY, *6*(3), 273–276

Activists Who Persevere

Donatella della Porta
Department of Political Science and Sociology
University of Florence

Why do people overcome self-interest and engage in a public cause? Who are the activists that join protest campaigns? Why does involvement sometimes survive even during the "low ebb" of a movement, when the excitement of mobilization evaporates? The question of individual commitment in collective action has been at the center of much theoretical reflection on its assumed rationality or irrationality, but not enough research has been devoted to the topic. Moreover, existing empirical analyses on political participation very often follow the tradition of survey studies. In their interesting book, James Downton and Paul Wehr start to fill this gap with a research based on 30 qualitative interviews of peace movement activists in Boulder and Denver, Colorado. In particular, they focus on the "personal attributes that contribute to long term activism" (p. 8), investigating the differences between the "*persisters*," that is, those who kept their commitment to the peace movement over time, the "*shifters*," that is, those who switched to other movements, and the "*dropouts,*" that is, those who retreated to private life.

The hypothesis of the volume is that "Social activism is similar to a normal career in many ways. A person must have the aptitude for the job, the career evolves in definite stages, and it persists because many personal and social factors maintain it" (pp. 13–14). Chapters are devoted to discussing different aspects of the "activist career": the ethical base for peace action, first involvement in the movement, the formation of a peace activist identity, personal empowerment related to activism, and solution to burnout problems.

Life-history interviews allow following the development of individual identities among peace activists. First of all, they indicate that, as neo-institutionalists

---

The Persistent Activist: How Peace Commitment Develops and Survives, James Downton and Paul Wehr, 1997, Boulder, CO: Westview Press.

Requests for reprints should be sent to Donatella della Porta, Dipartimento di scienza della politica e sociologia, Via Valori 9 50132 Firenze, Italy. E-mail: dellaporta@unifi.it

would put it, behaviors are based on norms, and they provide rich materials to understand what are the standards for appropriate action in the community of peace activists. As the authors summarize, "peace activism is an ethical career which develops over time. It is ethical because it is guided by moral principles, such as loving your neighbor, resolving conflicts without violence, and creating communities based on mutual respect, equality, cooperation, and social justice" (p. 17). Experiences in the family as well as in the educational system play an important role in an early socialization to values such as social justice, community involvement, and personal responsibility. But it is especially in the movements of the 60s and the 70s—in the civil rights movements, in the student movement, in the anti-Vietnam war movement, the environmental movement, and the women's movement—that the value system of persisters was formed. Not by chance a strong majority of the interviewees belong to the "protest generation" (as many as 76% are over 30 years old). Attitudinal propensities are then strengthened by participation, up to the development of an "inability to visualize their life without peace action," the feeling that "working for peace and social change was what they were meant to do" (p. 14).

Attitudinal availability interacts with situational availability (flexible careers, part-time jobs, no children) in facilitating involvement. External circumstances function then as catalysts and transform moral concerns into political activism. It is important to notice, however, that the activists themselves often forge situational availability. Everyday life—family as well as job arrangements—is organized to make it compatible with political activism. Their professional choices reflect their political choices: many of the interviewees work in the "helping professions" (social workers, health workers, etc.), they take part-time jobs to have time to devote to activism, sometimes they have a paid occupation in peace activities (nonviolence training, mediation service), and they are highly educated, but "their income distribution tends towards the low end of the scale" (p. 11). In other words, after they joined the peace movement, "they tended to structure their life so as to be freer for peace action" (p. 37).

Political opportunities, such as historical events or opportunities for political involvement in the community, help transform ideological inclinations and situational availability into action. The presence of local peace groups and ongoing campaigns against a local target allow people to act. Here too, however, the activists themselves influence the available opportunities, insofar as they invest their capacity to organize in the organization of collective action—in fact, as the authors rightly recall, "during the 1970s the people who turned to social activism learned to participate in everything from street politics to public policy hearings" (p. 41). With their activism, they force the system to become more open to the pressure from below. Moreover, the activist identity filters the external circumstances, with a high sensitivity for singling out new challenges.

Persisters share an optimistic view of the effect of their action. The movement is perceived as successful. Notwithstanding some sense of frustration, the activists are confident in the capacity of the movement to have a positive impact, in particular by introducing gradual changes in a long-term development. In fact, they share a vision of "a peace process building over decades and centuries, the results of innumerable individual efforts" (p. 75). The role of the activists is, first of all, a personal witness for their peace vision. As an activist put it, "We witness peace and maybe even we are peace and that has a real influence" (p. 75).

Personal ties inside the organizations are strong predictors for the maintenance of commitment. Commitment is in fact strengthened by affective ties with members of the same movement: "Close friendships are the heart of community, forged by countless hours of working together" (p. 64). Friends are selected along ideological lines. Together with competing responsibility, the lack of strong affective ties within the peace activist community is the only remarkable characteristic of dropouts in comparison with persisters.

This research on peace activists confirms some dynamics already noticed in different times and places. Doug McAdam's work on civil right activists in the United States, Florence Passy's work on the activists of the solidarity movement in Switzerland, and my own work on left-wing radicals in Italy, all converge in indicating the importance of shared belief, strong friendship ties, and socially constructed realities in forming activist identities (see, for example, della Porta, 1995; McAdam, 1988; & Passy, 1998). Movements are, in this sense, made of communities that produce and reinforce norms that are, to a certain extent, different from those that prevail in the larger society. Commitment is not the outcome of some causal variables, but a process, a "career," in which individuals are active players: they forge opportunities and they develop new values. As Downton and Wehr's book confirms, in-depth interviews are an invaluable instrument for understanding this process.

If participation in different movements shares similar dynamics, it is, however, maybe time to start to reflect on the differences between movements in different times and places. If activists construct *new* norms and codes of behavior, these norms and codes seem, however, different for different movements. The peace movement activists in the United State of the 90s stress the value of helping others in the community, nonviolent conflict resolution, gradual change, and personal witness. These values are *not* shared by all movements, not even in the so-called "left-libertarian" movement family. Quite the opposite, the movements of the 60s and the 70s emphasized the importance of fast, revolutionary transformation. Concepts such as "community" or "helping the others" are still considered with much skepticism by the European Left. More research is needed to systematically compare the normative systems of different movements, their origins, and their effects in terms of the construction of civic, democratic identities.

REFERENCES

della Porta, D. (1995). *Social movements, political violence and the state.* New York: Cambridge University Press.

McAdam, D. (1988). *Freedom summer.* New York: Oxford University Press.

Passy, F. (1998). *L'action altruiste: Contraintes et opportunites de l'engagement dans les mouvements sociaux.* Geneve: Droz.

PEACE AND CONFLICT: JOURNAL OF PEACE PSYCHOLOGY, *6*(3), 277–279

Globalism or Globaloney?

Ronnie D. Lipschutz
Department of Politics
University of California, Santa Cruz

> The bourgeoisie, by the rapid improvement of all instruments of production, by the immensely facilitated means of communication, draws all, even the most backward, nations into civilization ... It compels all nations, on the pain of extinction, to adopt the bourgeois mode of production; it compels them to introduce what it calls civilization into their midst, i.e., to become bourgeois themselves. In one word, it creates a world in its own image.
>
> Karl Marx, *The Communist Manifesto* (Marx & Engels, 1964, pp. 64–65).

What, exactly, is this "globalization" that has so captured the attention of policymakers, academics, and public alike? Is it something new, as many believers would have it, or is it merely another cycle in what is, by now, a 200-year history of industrial and economic change? Does globalization presage the end of state sovereignty and the international state system as it has been known since the Treaty of Westphalia, or does it enhance state control and power? Are markets and capital now in the driver's seat, as some claim, or could states regain control? Does anyone really know? And does it really matter? Over the past few years, the literature on globalization has grown at a rate comparable to the appreciation of high-tech equity prices on the NASDAQ stock exchange. Whether this textual bull market has provided as much enlightenment to analysts and academics as "dot-com" ideas have provided wealth to entrepreneurs and e-traders is less obvious. The two books under review help to shed some light on globalization, but they do not illuminate its full reach or implications.

Hirst and Thompson, in a revised and expanded version of their 1996 book, come to the subject from a skeptical leftist perspective. For them, "true" globalization would be restricted to the economic sphere, and would involve a clearly

---

Globalization in Question: The International Economy and the Possibilities of Governance (2nd ed.), 1999, Paul Hirst & Grahame Thompson. Cambridge, England: Polity Press.

Predatory Globalization—A Critique, 1999, Richard Falk. Cambridge, England: Polity Press.

Requests for reprints should be sent to Ronnie D. Lipschutz, Department of Politics, 260 Stevenson College, University of California, Santa Cruz, CA 95064. E-mail: rlipsch@cats.ucsc.edu

discernable movement toward full integration of formerly national (and somewhat autonomous) economies. Suffice it to say that they have marshaled considerable statistical evidence to convince themselves, and skeptics of globalization, that economic "internationalization" is moving toward a point comparable to that reached during the heyday of the Gold Standard in the late 19th and early 20th centuries. At the same time, however, we have yet to achieve that level (which, perhaps not coincidentally, culminated in World War I). In other words, there is nothing new about the current state of affairs. Hirst and Thompson identify tendencies toward full globalization, to be sure, but they argue that such a state of affairs remains off in a future that might never come to pass. For the moment, they seem to assert, globalization stands as a form of "false consciousness" used by politicians and capitalists alike to undermine the sorry remnants of the post-World War II welfare state and to justify policies that give greater freedom to capital and speculation.

Richard Falk is less concerned with the kinds of numbers bandied about by Hirst and Thompson (and there are lots of numbers) and is more anxious about the tendencies, especially as they seem to undermine both democracy and the general public welfare. Globalization, for Falk, is shorthand for a series of moves, by the politically powerful and the predatorily wealthy, to gain access to enhanced opportunities for accumulation. This, he fears, is leading to a world in which the everyday conditions of life will come to more closely approximate the Hobbesian state of nature than the Kantian world of liberal peace. There are alternatives to this grim future, writes Falk, but these rest on the political mobilization and activity of a "global civil society" that will strive for a democratic and more just form of global governance.

Both of these books are informative and provocative, and certainly part of the corpus of reading necessary to acquire a full understanding of globalization, but neither really examines the phenomenon from a critical perspective. Hirst and Thompson hope that, by demonstrating globalization to be a form of false consciousness, the left may be reenergized to challenge the conventional wisdom that all forms of socialism and social democracy are in the dustbins of history. The state lives! Falk believes that globalization is here, but that there are alternative forms of globalization, some much more democratic than others. Progressives have no choice but to challenge the more predatory versions.

A more critical, postpositivist analysis would suggest that globalization is a social construction, with both material and ideological components, whose actual significance is to be found at two different levels. First, a real reorganization of capitalist production is underway, due in no small part to the "electronics revolution," and this is having a major impact on social structures and transnational interactions. As various kinds of skills and social arrangements are devalued, because they are "inefficient" or insufficiently remunerative, customary ways of living and working are being broken apart, with concomitant disruption of peoples' lives. Second, the norms underlying this reorganization of social relations compel people to act in particular ways out of fear that they will be left behind if they do not. It is this that gives globalization its seeming inevitability. When the mantra of the day is "compete or die," few will want to take the chance of not going with the flow, and they will struggle to keep up with the rapidly-changing currents of globalization. But many are likely to fail, and even drown, so to speak, while the haves continue to paddle merrily down the stream.

REFERENCES

Marx, K., & Engels, F. (1964). *The Communist manifesto*. New York: Pocket Books.

Our idea of freedom is different from that of the reactionaries who talk of elections but not of social justice. Without social justice, democracy is not possible, for without it men would be slaves of poverty.

John Dewey, 1939

PEACE AND CONFLICT: JOURNAL OF PEACE PSYCHOLOGY, *6*(3), 281–284

The Psychology of Being Overtaken by Events

Benjamin E. Goldsmith
Department of Political Science
University of Michigan

Of the many descriptions of United States–Soviet relations during the final decade of Soviet power, Don Oberdorfer's book, *The Turn: From the Cold War to a New Era: The United States and the Soviet Union, 1983–1990* (1991), now in an updated Johns Hopkins edition, remains especially useful because it is both very well informed and relatively balanced. The veteran *Washington Post* reporter bases his account on extensive interviews, privileged access to meeting transcripts, and on memoirs and other published firsthand sources. Oberdorfer is to be commended most for resisting, with a few lapses, the temptation to give ad hoc interpretations of the events he describes. Because of this clear focus on accurately conveying "what happened and what it was like at the time" (p. 12), his book provides a reliable source of raw data for those interested in studying these important episodes in world politics from a variety of perspectives.

From the Cold War to a New Era tells the story of high-level diplomacy between the United States and the U.S.S.R. It follows negotiations and policy shifts on issues such as arms control, human rights, trade, and economic aid, including detailed accounts of summits and ministerial meetings throughout the period.

From the perspective of political psychology, there are a number of interesting areas for research suggested by the account. Oberdorfer proposes one himself: the power of the personalities of "remarkable human actors" for explaining major international realignments, or "turning points" (pp. 10–11). But this approach does not seem the most promising, and Oberdorfer himself qualifies it heavily. Topics such as the role of personal trust between negotiators, varying perceptions of real-

---

From the Cold War to a New Era: The United States and the Soviet Union, 1983–1991 (Updated ed.), Don Oberdorfer, 1998, Baltimore: The Johns Hopkins University Press.

Requests for reprints should be sent to Benjamin E. Goldsmith, Department of Political Science, University of Michigan, Ann Arbor, MI 48109. E-mail: goldsmib@umich.edu

ity, the tendency to project one's own concerns onto others, and the prominent role of analogical reasoning are areas at least as interesting for those seeking to study the impact of cognitive factors in international relations.

Oberdorfer's account seems to leave little question of the importance placed by all of the major players on developing personal, trusting relationships. Most notably, the relationship between Soviet Foreign Minister Eduard Shevardnadze and U.S. Secretary of State George Shultz was deliberately cultivated, and valued by both men. Soviet leader Mikhail Gorbachev and U.S. President Ronald Reagan are also reported to have considered their personal relationship a major factor in the development of United States–Soviet relations. In contrast, the pause in high-level contacts after George Bush became president resulted in a failure to build such relationships with the other side. Bush and his secretary of state, James Baker, did not determine the basic direction of U.S. policy toward the Soviets until they had established similar relationships with their Soviet counterparts. In spite of a wide-ranging and exhaustive multiagency review of U.S. Soviet policy, the evidence presented by Oberdorfer indicates that the basic direction of policy was set later, by the personal dynamics between the leaders.

The variation in the actors' perceptions of reality is also noteworthy. In particular, U.S. officials tended to regard the Soviet system as an obvious failure economically, politically, and morally; a system that was clearly inferior in all respects to the West. The very sight of Moscow's decaying infrastructure, or the fact of religious repression, was enough to confirm these views for Reagan or Baker, for example. Not surprisingly, the Soviets did not judge their society in such categorical terms. They recognized faults, but also felt that many of their socialist values had proven themselves, and were to be preferred to those of the West. Even as the U.S.S.R. crumbled, neither Gorbachev nor Shevardnadze abandoned a basic belief in socialism. Facts may be stubborn things, but humans' ability to give them a bewilderingly wide range of interpretations is also an enduring phenomenon. And it affects the behavior of political actors.

Although perceptions may have differed, there is also evidence that each side tried to stay well informed about the domestic-level constraints facing the other. Rarely did any of the major players fall into the easy mental habit of perceiving one's opponent as a monolithic unity of action and purpose. Gorbachev's interpretation of U.S. domestic politics evolved from vague ideas about the military industrial complex or Bechtel corporation (where both Shultz and Defense Secretary Carlucci had worked), to specific assumptions about the beliefs of the electorate, and even direct lobbying of U.S. legislators (live on CNN, no less) in 1990. The often-criticized U.S. policy of overt support for Gorbachev personally, especially under Bush, was driven by an increasing awareness of divisions within the Politburo, the Soviet military, and other institutions in the U.S.S.R.

If one takes his public and private statements at face value, Gorbachev had a consistent tendency to project the challenges facing the U.S.S.R., and his policies responding to them, onto the United States. Although the Soviet Union was changing, nothing fundamental about U.S. policy was, other than its recognition of Soviet reform in domestic and international politics. Gorbachev, however, referred to the process as one of "the two sides ... find[ing] a way out of the prison of old stereotypes, away from imposing our own approaches and views on each other" (p. 284). This contrasts sharply with the U.S. position. Shultz, for example, stated bluntly to Reagan in 1986, "You know the Soviet Union is not in our class economically or in terms of human values" (p. 172). Although Gorbachev believed that the U.S. had come around to "a more correct and tolerant perception of my country" (p. 271), the view on the United States side was that only the Soviet Union had changed, with help from the United States and at least in part in response to U.S. pressure. Bush concisely summarized the U.S. perspective in his 1989 statement that "Containment worked ... " (p. 347). Perhaps Gorbachev's statements were merely face-saving rhetoric, but I tend to think that he believed them.

The prominent role of analogical reasoning in the public statements, and more importantly, in the private deliberations of decision makers is evident throughout the book. Analogies are used not only rhetorically, but also to communicate real beliefs. Soviet reforms were driven at least in part by reference to Japan's postwar economic success, and the stark contrast of the performance of the Soviet system over the same period. Lithuanian leaders saw the failure of the West to support their 1990 drive for independence as another "Munich" (p 404). Both United States and Soviet leaders frequently used the U.S. experience in Vietnam to frame their understanding of the U.S.S.R.'s war in Afghanistan. These analogies probably do reveal powerful schemas that influenced the basic direction of policies.

This updated edition includes a final chapter covering mid-1990 through the end of 1991 (and of the U.S.S.R.). An appendix that was in the first edition (1991) has been omitted, although it is still referenced in the text. The publisher also deserves criticism for some annoying typographical errors and lower-quality reproductions of photographs than those in the first edition. A more substantive criticism of Oberdorfer's new chapter is that it relies heavily on Gorbachev's published account of the 1991 coup, but does not warn the reader of this.

Although overall Oberdorfer clearly attempts to give a balanced account, the large amount of information obtained from the U.S. participants does tend to drive the narrative. In particular, the apparent close cooperation of George Shultz, who gave Oberdorfer 13 interviews, may introduce some bias. Nevertheless, Oberdorfer has done an impressive job of securing interviews and documents from Soviet participants in these events as well.

But these relatively minor faults do not overshadow the overall reliability of the sources, and the detail and apparent accuracy of the narration. These attributes make Oberdorfer's book a rare and valuable commodity. It suggests many potentially profitable avenues of research, some of which I have attempted to describe here in a cursory way. Of course, comparison with other cases, and with other sources on these same events, must precede any conclusions. Two new books may be especially useful in this regard: Angela Stent's (1999) account of German and Soviet/Russian diplomacy during roughly the same period, and the Russian-language memoirs of Valentin Falin (1999), an important figure in Soviet foreign policy under Gorbachev.

One conclusion I will suggest is that the principal actors were unable to change their basic schemas quickly enough to keep up with the shifting reality of East–West relations. This is especially evident on the Soviet side during the processes of German unification and Soviet disintegration. The Bush administration's tenacity in clinging to Cold War strategies is also noteworthy in this regard. What Oberdorfer calls "underlying trends" undoubtedly overtook the policymakers who were attempting to shape United States–Soviet relations. In the absence of well-worn cognitive tools to fit a situation, "leaders" can easily become followers of events, driven by forces they are poorly equipped to understand.

REFERENCES

Falin, V. (1999). *Konflikty v Kremle: Sumerki bogov po-russki* [Conflicts in the Kremlin: Twilight of the gods, Russian style]. Moscow: Tsentrpoligraf.

Oberdorfer. D. (1991). *The turn: From the Cold War to a new era: The United States and the Soviet Union, 1983–1990.* New York: Simon & Schuster.

Stent, A. (1999). *Russia and Germany reborn: Unification, the Soviet collapse, and the new Europe.* Princeton, NJ: Princeton University Press.

PEACE AND CONFLICT: JOURNAL OF PEACE PSYCHOLOGY, *6*(3), 285–287

Are We Imprisoned Within Culture?

Michael Huspek
Communication Program
California State University, San Marcos

Avruch argues that cultural analysis should be "an irreducible part of problem solving" (p. 98) and introduces a concept of culture "as an analytical tool for understanding conflict and conflict resolution" (p. 16). Culture, Avruch stresses, is not reducible to a single, homogenous, unchanging tradition or custom, and it is not likely to be dispersed throughout the membership of a social group in uniform ways. Rather, culture consists of experientially derived "images and encodements, schemas and models" (p. 19), more or less organized, either learned or created by individuals. Culture is complex, fluid, and may constitute only one of many cultures distributed across the social landscape.

On this definition, individuals are viewed as being more than simply strategic game players or utility maximizers. As cultural beings, they may vary in their ability to successfully integrate the resources of one or more cultures into their overall cognitive makeup; so, too, the groups or institutions that they may represent. An institution such as the political state, for example, is more than a monolithic set of interests or cultural values. And, by the same reasoning, the relationship of individuals to the groups or institutions they represent may not always be of simple one-to-one correspondence.

Avruch does a credible job of showing how current theories and methods in the field of conflict resolution might profit from a greater sensitivity to the culture concept, and the book deserves to be read on this count alone. However, the overall thesis is impaired by the author's tendency to treat personality traits, individual stylistics, and perhaps all forms of knowledge as cultural phenomena, and then to gloss over theoretical questions that are likely to crop up in response to such

---

Culture and Conflict Resolution, Kevin Avruch, 1998, Washington, DC: United States Institute of Peace Press.

Requests for reprints should be sent to Michael Huspek, Communication Program, California State University, San Marcos, CA 92096–0001. E-mail: mhuspek@coyote.csusm.edu

reductionism. Where, for example, does one culture stop and another begin? How do we know whether one's speech offerings are grounded in one culture as opposed to another culture? How can we begin to critically discuss and reflect on culture if we ourselves are trapped entirely within our own cultural skins? Failure to address such questions renders suspect the utility of the culture concept for analyzing the motives, influences, or manifestations of conflict.

Such questions are no less relevant as Avruch shifts from analysis of conflict to discussions of the pragmatics of conflict resolution. Regarding the latter, Avruch relies on the culture concept to recommend against prescriptive models. All too often, he asserts, such models are defined by "one's own (typically North American and middle class) presumptions about conflict and third-party roles [being] elevated to the status of expert system" (p.97). As a preferred alternative, Avruch offers what he calls an elicitive approach wherein meanings emerge in an atmosphere of mutual discovery. With this approach he believes "something like a new culture" may come about (p.99).

Avruch's elicitive approach itself contains some prescriptive elements. For example, he implicitly endorses openness, flexibility, and, perhaps most important, a willingness to engage in "unhampered communication" (p.96). Avruch does not define such terms, however, perhaps fearing that he too will fall sway to the expert's temptation to foist one or another hegemonic mapping on otherwise culturally disparate individuals. Nevertheless, absent such definitions, there appears to be no guarantee that communication between parties must proceed in the direction of mutual discovery and sharing of insight that Avruch so desires.

Consider the presence of power that, Avruch laments, "remains problematical for conflict resolution theorists" (p.55). It simply is not clear how his culture concept or its derived elicitive model makes power any less problematical. What is the active participant or third party mediator to do should an interlocutor refuse to acknowledge the desirability of mutual discovery and shared insight? This may be more than simply a cultural problem where, to draw on Alasdair MacIntyre's metaphor, "moving one's knight to QB3 may be replied to with a lob across the net"; for some participants may attempt to capitalize intentionally on asymmetrical possession of material or symbolic resources in the relationship. Rather than proceeding with good will toward mutual discovery and shared insight within an elicitive environment where consensus is the ideal, one's intended goal in fact may be to derail any such undertaking by whatever communicative means.

The elicitive approach advanced by Avruch may be useful when parties to conflict resolution act on a genuine willingness to engage in open, flexible, and unhampered communication. But in the many cases when such dispositions are lacking—that is, when interactants operate on bad faith, deception, or a strategic unwillingness to work toward consensus—Avruch offers no procedural rules or guidelines that might effectively counter a power-holder's attempts to trump another at each and every turn.

In the final analysis, Avruch's unwillingness to develop procedures or rules for dispute cases is disappointing. Can we not assume that some ways of engaging in conflict resolution are preferable to others? Are we not capable of acquiring more knowledgeable ways of minimizing the negative effects of power imbalances within conflict resolution arenas? Given Avruch's suggestion that openness, flexibility, and unhampered communication are preferable to their opposites, further investigation into the epistemological grounds for such standards and how one might then argue for their rationality over and above what may be culturally specific claims to the contrary is needed.

...those old-fashioned animal ambitions for mastery and mere success which seem now to be sweeping away the world, and us at the wake. This is the real and concrete spring of action, it seems to me, that is exciting us; and raising and educating inferior races, is mere hollow protest and unreality...

William James, 1899

PEACE AND CONFLICT: JOURNAL OF PEACE PSYCHOLOGY, *6*(3), 289–290

Against War

Frances B. McCrea
Department of Sociology
Grand Valley State University

When Lawrence Wittner published *Rebels Against War* in 1984, it was clearly the most comprehensive and best study of the peace movement available. For a decade, it remained the standard. With this projected three volume *magnum opus*, *The Struggle Against the Bomb*, Wittner partially supplants his older volume. His focus is narrowed, to be sure, but the analysis is also broadened in this study of the worldwide protest against nuclear weapons.

In Volume I, *One World or None*, published in 1993, Wittner examined the opposition to the atomic bomb that arose from the Manhattan Project as well as the postwar efforts to control nuclear weapons. The subject of this review is Volume Two, *Resisting the Bomb*, which covers the fascinating period from 1954 to 1970.

The book has three obvious strengths. First, Wittner does not limit his focus to the American scene. For a technology that can destroy the world, his story is appropriately and ambitiously global. Although the narrative centers on the United States, Western Europe, and Japan, other countries (Third World included) are not ignored. Second, Wittner's prose is not only graceful, but also precise. He knows how to tell a story, no mean feat for this complex of disparate actions (sometimes causally related, sometimes not) that happen across the face of the earth. Third, Wittner tells his story with extensive documentation, much of which has been declassified or released (on both sides of the iron curtain) only in recent years.

To illustrate this richness, I consider one example. I found that the story of SANE, and its chief protagonists, was told comprehensively. Wittner captured quite well the terrible (and ultimately unsolvable) problems faced by Norman Cousins and others during the McCarthy years: how to advocate an anti-establishment position

---

The Struggle Against the Bomb, Volume Two. Resisting the Bomb: A History of the World Nuclear Disarmament Movement, 1954–1970, 1997, Lawrence S. Wittner. Stanford, CA: Stanford University Press.

Cultures of Antimilitarism: National Security in Germany and Japan, 1998, Thomas U. Berqer. Baltimore: Johns Hopkins University Press.

Requests for reprints should be sent to Frances B. McCrea, Department of Sociology, Grand Valley State University, Allendale, MI 49401. E-mail: McCreaf@gvsu.edu

while keeping a distance from the left (particularly anything even distantly resembling the Communist party position). So far, so good. But Wittner enriches his analysis by comparing and contrasting SANE's problems with a series of case studies of like-minded movements around the world (including less known examples from countries such as Greece and Brazil).

This volume concludes with the decline of the peace movement from 1964 to 1970. I eagerly await the publication of Volume III, to follow the story of the worldwide Freeze movement that seemed to hold such promise, only to flounder, as had its predecessors.

Amidst this positive reaction, I have only two reservations. First, because this is a so-called "internalist" history, one gets little sense of the great nation–states that stand powerfully above, and in opposition to, this movement. Thus, readers might wonder why SANE and like-minded movements ended in what can only be judged as failures. Second, a strength can be a weakness. For in the insistence on telling all stories in all countries, the focus is sometimes momentarily lost.

Thomas Berger's book, *Cultures of Antimilitarism*, pairs nicely with Wittner's. The study focuses on Germany and Japan, both of which achieved economic dominance and political influence in the post-World War II world. Both countries have armed forces of substantial size and potency, and neither is pacifist. Then why is it, the author asks, that these two powerful nations are strongly antimilitaristic? The question is a good one, but Berger quickly (too quickly, I think) rejects economic and geopolitical explanations.

Rather, Berger relies on the theory of political culture. The body of the book argues that in both postwar countries, right–center governments, in alliance with intellectuals, were able to engage in culture-building and craft new national identities. Accordingly, the two countries are antimilitarist because each attempted to "draw lessons from its troubled past" (p. 6). To construct this argument, Berger uses a wide variety of secondary sources as well as numerous interviews with contemporary political actors.

This is an appealing explanation. But, like all studies that rely on the concept of political culture, Berger's surely minimizes the long-run of history. The biggest problem, it seems to me, is that the author accepts the notion and very meaning of culture (hotly debated in many circles), *sui generis*. Indeed, if culture is so nonproblematic, then it is difficult to imagine such a radical change from the prewar to the postwar period. And, if culture does change so dramatically, then perhaps it is wise to consider the notion more as a result than a cause of things.

Berger concludes that German and Japanese antimilitarism will fade slowly. "Even the external shock of the Gulf War by itself was of insufficient magnitude to overcome their deeply sedimented antimilitarist values" (p. 192). Yet even before the publication of this book, although certainly after its writing, the activist role of the German military in the breakup of Yugoslavia (particularly in the so-called "peacekeeping") mitigates this gradualist thesis.